INSIGHT

CW00921100

CUBa

DISCOVERY
CHANNEL

APA PUBLICATIONS
Part of the Langenscheidt Publishing Group

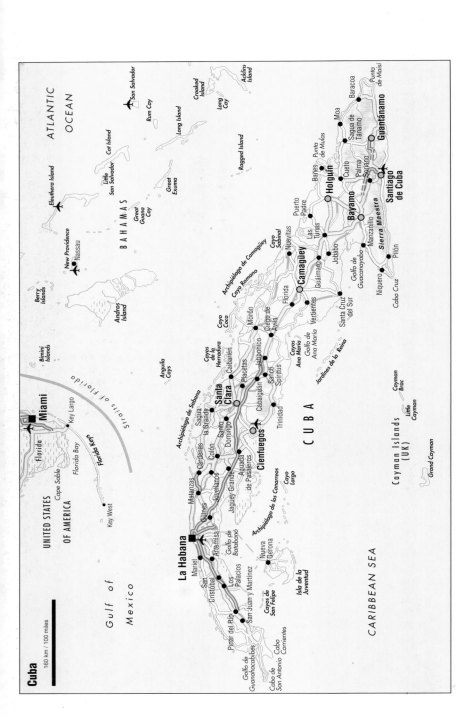

Cuba

160 km / 100 miles

introduction

Welcome

This is one of 133 itinerary-based *Pocket Guides* produced by the editors of Insight Guides, whose books have set the standard for visual travel guides since 1970. With top-quality photography and authoritative recommendations, this guidebook aims to help visitors with limited time experience the many different aspects of the island and get the most out of their stay.

The author, Danny Aeberhard, has devised a series of itineraries linking the highlights of the country. They start in Havana with four tours, focusing first on Old Havana, radiating from the cathedral; then Central Havana, with its Fine Art and Revolutionary museums; Vedado, the business district; and lastly the area around Havana, including Ernest Hemingway's former home in the southern suburb of San Francisco de Paula. The remaining nine tours explore the rest of the island, moving first to the tobacco-growing area in western Cuba, then to Central Cuba, including the Zapata Peninsula, Trinidad, Santa Clara, Remedios and Camagüey, and lastly the east (El Oriente), exploring Santiago de Cuba, the road to Baracoa (passing Guantánamo Bay) and taking an adventurous round trip of the Sierra Maestra, a rugged coastal range of mountains. Supporting the itineraries are sections on history and culture, shopping, eating out, nightlife and festivals, plus a round-up of Cuba's finest beaches. Lastly, there is a fact-packed useful practical information chapter, including a list of recommended hotels at a range of price levels, advice on getting around, money matters, etc.

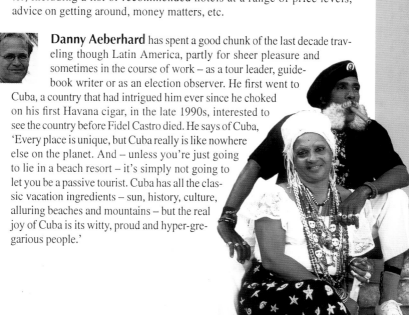

Danny Aeberhard has spent a good chunk of the last decade traveling though Latin America, partly for sheer pleasure and sometimes in the course of work – as a tour leader, guidebook writer or as an election observer. He first went to Cuba, a country that had intrigued him ever since he choked on his first Havana cigar, in the late 1990s, interested to see the country before Fidel Castro died. He says of Cuba, 'Every place is unique, but Cuba really is like nowhere else on the planet. And – unless you're just going to lie in a beach resort – it's simply not going to let you be a passive tourist. Cuba has all the classic vacation ingredients – sun, history, culture, alluring beaches and mountains – but the real joy of Cuba is its witty, proud and hyper-gregarious people.'

History & Culture

Cuba's history is suitably tropical – periods of relative calm interrupted by great hurricanes of violence and political turbulence. The first humans to reach the Cuban mainland were hunter-gatherer groups. Island-hopping through the Caribbean, they had arrived on the mainland by 3500BC. There have been attempts to classify them into different ethnic groups, such as Guanahatabeyes and Ciboneyes, but they now tend to be classified merely as being pre-agricultural and pre-ceramic cultures.

These cultures were later influenced by Taíno Arawak groups who had their origins in the Orinoco region (in modern Venezuela), and reached mainland Cuba from about AD600. The Taínos had advanced agricultural techniques, were skilled potters and had a rich ceremonial and spiritual life. They came to dominate the western and central regions of Cuba, although Ciboney hunter-gatherer groups continued to survive in all areas of the island. Pre-Columbian demographics is an inexact science, but modern estimates put the indigenous population in Cuba at the time of the European explorers' arrival at the end of the 15th century at around 150,000.

The Devil in Eden

The initial contact with Europeans was peaceful. When Christopher Columbus first touched Cuban soil, in October 1492, any greed he and his crew may have had was tempered by curiosity and wonder. Indeed, he described this land – which he believed to be China – as a veritable Eden, the most beautiful land that eyes had set on, peopled by gentle, laughing natives.

When Diego Velázquez de Cuéllar sailed across from what is now the Dominican Republic to begin Spanish settlement in 1511, he and his men brought with them a Christian God, but their behavior was most un-Christian in its brutality. Bartolomé de Las Casas, the priest who accompanied them, described one scene when a group of Taínos came down to offer gifts, bread and fish to his compatriots: '*Suddenly the Devil rose up in the Spanish, and they put to the sword – in my presence and with no motive whatsoever – more than 3,000 souls who were seated in front of us, men, women and children.*'

Resistance to the Spaniards was led by a Taíno *cacique* (chief) named Hatuey, who had fled the barbarism of the Spanish in Haiti. Finally captured, he was tied to the stake to be burned alive. A priest gave him the chance to accept God, and thus attain heaven. Hatuey asked the priest if there were Christians in heaven and, when told that indeed there were, responded that he'd prefer to go to hell rather than a place where there were people of such cruelty.

Left: an idealized picture of slavery
Right: Christopher Columbus

The indigenous population went into freefall, and not merely because of massacres by the *conquistadores*. Mass suicide and new European diseases laid whole communities to waste.

Spain's Pearl of the Antilles

By the mid-16th century, only a few thousand indigenous people remained alive and the Spanish colony was growing fast. The first seven towns founded by Velázquez and his settlers – Baracoa, Bayamo, Havana, Puerto del Príncipe (present-day Camagüey), Santiago, Sancti Spíritus and Trinidad – were beginning to prosper, despite attacks from corsairs. The Spanish had brought black slaves from Africa – first as domestic servants and then to replace the dying indigenous laborers in the gold mines and the fields. Gradually, the economy started to grow, and the colonists earned a decent living through exporting tobacco, sugar, dried meats, leather and precious hardwoods.

Havana, too, was coming to prominence. Sited on the Gulf Stream, it was ideally placed to provision the fleets that sailed from Mexico, Panama and Colombia, laden with New World bullion, before catching the trade winds that would blow them toward Seville. This made the port a particular prize and in 1762 Havana was taken by an Anglo-American force under the Earl of Albermarle. During their occupation, the port was opened up to free trade. In return for ceding Florida to the English, the Spanish Crown regained sovereignty of Havana in 1763 but found it difficult to reimpose its monopolistic ways on the *habaneros*. This English legacy paved the way for the next sea of change in Cuban life – the era of slavery on a massive scale, designed to provide the workforce for a booming sugar plantation economy.

Slavers scrambled to pack captive Africans into their holds: among them Lucumí and Yoruba peoples from West Africa, and Bantú groups from the

Congo basin and Angola. Thousands died on the journey, but those that survived brought with them African religions, dance and music, which have all had a profound influence on Cuban culture. This often painful fusion of Spanish colonial and African cultures is the bedrock of Cuban society. Soon to emerge were syncretic religions such as Santería – widespread today – where African gods are worshipped through, and alongside, Catholic saints. Cuba's vibrant music, meanwhile, was once famously described by ethnographer Fernando Ortiz as 'a love affair between the Spanish guitar and the African drum.'

Above: statue of Hautey. **Left:** Mambí independence fighters take on the Spanish

Struggle for Independence

The independence movements of the 19th-century were taken up in Cuba on October 10, 1868, when the sugar plantation owner Carlos Manuel de Céspedes summoned his workers together, freed his slaves and issued a call to arms, raising the cry of 'Independence or Death.' The First War of Independence had begun – a slow-burning war that dragged on for 10 years before being snuffed out by the Spanish. It shattered the country's economy, and the resulting low land prices attracted American investors. Most of the surviving independence leaders fled into exile.

Emancipation came in 1886, by which time slavery was no longer politically or economically viable.

Meanwhile, abroad, exiles continued to advocate passionately for Cuban independence. Leading the effort was the writer and poet, José Martí, who plotted with such heroes of the first war as generals Máximo Gómez and Antonio Maceo. In 1895, these men landed in the east of Cuba to fight the Spanish once again. Martí, the soldier-poet, was shot dead in one of the first skirmishes and his martyrdom has made him a hero to Cubans of all political persuasions. Maceo also fell in combat, but the moustachioed Gómez continued the fight and by 1898 Cuban forces seemed to be gaining the upper hand.

At this point, the United States, which had advocated the annexation or purchase of Cuba at various times in the past and feared for its investments, stepped into the conflict, setting the tone for US-Cuban relations through much of the next century. By the end of 1898, the Spanish were defeated, but the peace deal cut out the Cubans completely, and the Spanish handed power to the US.

Before US forces withdrew, a new constitution had been drafted including the notorious Platt Amendment, which gave the US the right to intervene in Cuban affairs and the right to lease on an indefinite basis a naval base -- Guantánamo.

Many Cubans felt they had been deprived of true independence just when they were at the point of victory, and the Platt Amendment aroused bitter resentment. The US military intervened again in Cuban affairs on three separate occasions over the next three decades, claiming to restore public order when in fact the prime motive was to secure their growing business interests.

Coups and Revolution

The first half of the 20th century saw a string of regimes come and go – many of them sponsored by Washington, and most of them memorable for their brutality. The most infamous was that of Gerardo Machado, a dictator whose repression earned him the hatred of his people.

After the fall of Machado in 1933, Fulgencio Batista, a mulatto army sergeant and the son of a cane-cutter, began to assume prominence in Cuban political affairs. Initially he was able to install puppet presidents, but soon he

Right: writer and poet José Martí, advocate of Cuban independence

was standing for election himself, serving his first term as President between 1944 and 1948. Batista took a reformist line, legislating on a number of issues to improve social justice, but the period also saw a growth of gangsterism and the rise of the US Mafia in Cuba.

The venality of subsequent regimes did nothing to alter the lot of the average Cuban, and when Batista seized power in a coup in 1952 reformists felt they had been robbed of their chance to clean up Cuban politics. A number of anti-Batista factions emerged in a volatile climate that saw Batista rely increasingly on political assassinations and the use of fear as instruments of control, while corruption grew ever more rampant. The Mafia made Cuba their playground, and much of 1950s Havana looked particularly glamorous, albeit set against a backdrop of prostitution and desperate poverty.

A young student activist, Fidel Castro Ruz, decided to act. In 1953, he and a band of supporters planned an attack to set the wheels of revolution in motion – an assault on Santiago's Moncada garrison. The episode was a disaster and Castro was captured. After a period of imprisonment, he left for exile in Mexico, where he was to meet a young Argentine doctor by the name of Ernesto 'Che' Guevara. Soon after, in December 1956, 82 men returned to Cuba in a secondhand pleasure craft called the *Granma*, named by the previous owner after his grandmother and now the centerpiece of the Museo de la Revolución in Havana. The force was largely obliterated within the first few disastrous days but a handful – including Che Guevara, Fidel and his brother Raúl Castro – survived to regroup in the Sierra Maestra mountains. The guerrilla forces gained strength, and by the end of 1958 they had Batista's demoralized troops in disarray.

Batista fled to the Dominican Republic, leaving the bearded revolutionaries to swagger into Havana in triumph, grinning from their open-top American roadsters.

The Revolution brought sweeping change, first of all with the passing of an Agrarian Reform Law that opened up land ownership, and then with the nationalization of infrastructure and foreign-owned businesses. This raised hackles in the US, and in 1960 President Eisenhower blocked imports of Cuban sugar, forcing the Cubans to look elsewhere for a market. They found a willing partner in the Soviet Union, and against the background of the Cold War, the US-Cuba spat escalated with frightening speed.

Above: Havana in the 1940s
Right: Fulgencia Batista

The disastrous Bay of Pigs invasion of April 1961 *(see page 43)* only served to underline Castro's belief that the US would stop at nothing to topple him. CIA-sponsored assassination plots did nothing to assuage the situation, and as relations soured, Castro moved ever farther to the left. By the end of the year, Castro had declared Cuba to be a Marxist-Leninist state and he sought military aid from the Soviet Union to deter any further US invasion. Tensions came to a head with the Cuban Missile Crisis in October 1962, the closest the world has ever come to full-scale nuclear war. Stepping back from the brink, Khrushchev eventually withdrew Soviet nuclear missiles from their tropical island bunkers and Cuba received US assurances that there would be no invasion.

Cuba was punching way above its weight on the world stage. Ironically, however, the country was in many ways in the same situation now as it had been before the Revolution: dependent on a monoculture plantation economy, but this time exporting to the Soviet Union, not the US.

This situation remained for the next quarter of a century until the socialist regimes of Eastern Europe and the Soviet Union imploded between 1989 and 1991 and Cuba was caught in the fallout. Russia withdrew all its subsidies, leaving Cuba to face economic meltdown. Castro's response to these crises was to announce the Special Period in Peacetime, a series of austerity measures the likes of which Cubans had never experienced before. Without subsidized oil imports from Russia, industry ground to a halt, and a million bicycles had to be imported from China to keep Cuba on the move.

Meanwhile, sensing that a tottering Castro might finally be forced from power, the US strengthened its economic blockade. This gave Castro the chance to play the victim, blaming the US blockade for Cuba's woes, and appealing to both Cubans' fierce nationalism and their long-standing resentment of what they see as bullying by their superpower neighbor. However, popular discontent demanded internal reform, too – limited private enterprise was permitted and, in 1993, in a move that must have wounded Castro's pride, the dollar was legalized to save the nation from bankruptcy.

Cuba limped through the 1990s, gradually rebuilding an economy that depended on tourism more than sugar exports.

Cuba Today

Cuba today is ethnically diverse – official figures show only 11 percent of the population is black, but unofficial estimates indicate that as many as 70 percent is of mixed race. Since the Revolution, more than a million – mainly white – people have fled Cuba to start a new life in Miami and Castro's

Above: Khrushchev and Castro greet one another

Cuba has embraced its black African heritage – some say out of necessity. Cuba is one of the few Latin American societies where you sense the population is generally at ease with its ethnic make up.

Today's Cuba has few traces of its indigenous background, short of a linguistic legacy. However, Cubans are proud of their history of rebellion, and identify with people like Hatuey for resisting the foreign invader. Indeed sovereignty and national pride are hallmarks of the country's culture.

Castro's Revolution has been a mixed experience for the people. It brought with it undoubted successes in the fields of education and health, and both life expectancy (74 years) and literacy rates (95 percent) are high given its poor economic indicators. However, the Cuban State can be incredibly repressive when it comes to individual freedoms that most in the West take for granted. In addition, whereas no one starves, most Cuban citizens are involved in a perpetual struggle – *luchando*, as they say – to get by.

The desperate austerity of the Special Period is no longer so noticeable: there are far more goods to buy in the stores than before the introduction of the dollar. However, with average wages significantly less than US$10 a month, few people can afford them; and the ration book *(libreta)* is still part of the average Cuban's life. Many resent the stifling of opportunity; others are passionate *Fidelistas*, tremendously proud of their country and its achievements.

The big questions about Cuba's future, however, remain unanswered – no one knows what will happen when Fidel Castro eventually dies or is forced from power. In the meantime, Cubans get on with the day-to-day business of making the most of life – a field in which, fortunately, they have boundless talent.

HISTORY HIGHLIGHTS

c. 3500BC First human settlement.

AD600–1000 Arrival of agricultural Taíno peoples.

1492 Columbus lands on Cuban soil.

1511 Diego Velázquez's expedition begins European settlement.

1517 First shipment of slaves from Africa.

1553 Capital moved from Santiago to Havana.

1555 French pirate Jacques de Sores burns Havana.

1628 Dutch privateer Piet Heyn captures Spanish treasure fleet at Matanzas.

1662 Englishman Sir Christopher Myngs sacks Santiago.

1711 Tobacco growers rebel against monopolistic policies of Spanish Crown.

1762–3 Earl of Albermarle's Anglo-American expedition occupies Havana.

1789 Trading restrictions on import of slaves lifted.

Early 1800s More than half the population is black.

1866 Slave trade outlawed

1868–1878 First War of Independence against Spain.

1886 Abolition of slavery in Cuba.

1895–8 Second War of Independence.

1895 José Martí killed.

1898 US enters war and defeats Spanish, who hand over power in the Treaty of Paris. Cubans excluded from the peace process.

1901 Constitution adopted with controversial Platt Amendment, giving the US the right to intervene in Cuban affairs.

1902 Tomás Estrada Palma becomes first president of Cuban Republic.

1903 Lease of Guantánamo begins.

1906–9 Second US intervention after uprising against Estrada Palma.

1925–1933 Dictator Gerardo Machado in power.

1928 Women get the vote.

1933–4 Fulgencio Batista emerges as dominant force in Cuban politics.

1940–4 Batista serves term as elected President.

1952 Batista seizes power in coup.

1953 Attack on Moncada garrison, led by Fidel Castro.

1956 Castro's revolutionaries land in the *Granma* to begin rebel war in the Sierra Maestra.

1958 Military gains by rebels.

1959 Batista flees to exile; triumph of Castro's revolutionary forces (January 1). Castro becomes Prime Minister. Agrarian Reform Law passed.

1960 Trade treaty signed with Soviet Union. Foreign-owned companies and banks nationalized.

1961 US breaks off diplomatic relations. Castro proclaims Socialist nature of Revolution. US-sponsored Bay of Pigs invasion fails.

1962 President Kennedy imposes economic embargo. Cuban Missile Crisis (October).

1968 Small private businesses confiscated.

1980 120,000 refugees leave for Miami during Mariel boatlift.

1991 Russian aid to Cuba axed.

1993–4 Worst economic hardship of the Special Period. Dollar legalised.

1994 40,000 refugees (*balseros*) flee Cuba for the US, prompting the US to end its open-door policy for Cuban immigrants.

1995 Foreign ownership of businesses allowed.

1996 Helms-Burton Act tightens US embargo, aiming to penalize foreign companies doing business in Cuba.

1998 Visit of Pope John Paul II.

1999 Stricter penalties on dissent.

2003 Crackdown on political dissidents brings worldwide criticism of Cuba's human rights record.

history/culture

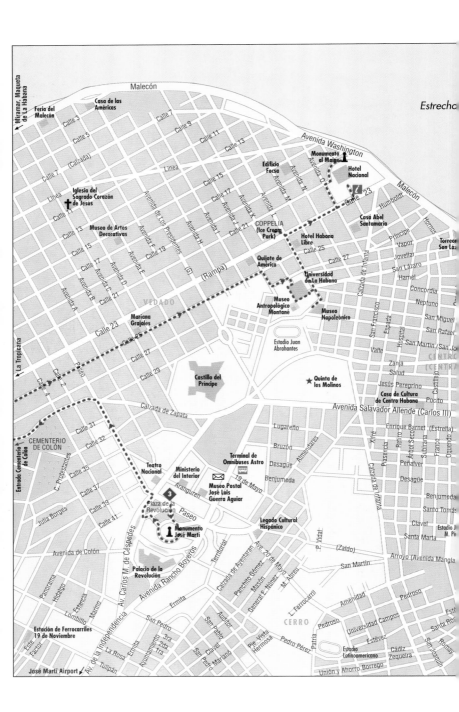

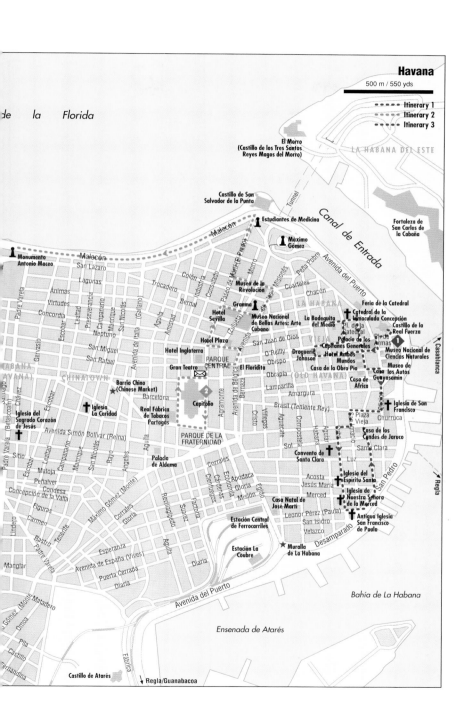

Orientation

The largest Caribbean island, Cuba is much longer than most people realize: 861km (535 miles) of road separate the two main cities, Havana and Santiago and, considering they're not always in tip-top condition, you can expect at least a 12-hour stretch of driving to cover the distance. Many people opt to fly.

Havana is Cuba's great metropolis, with a population of more than 2 million, and the city will be, in all likelihood, the place you enter and leave Cuba. Four of the itineraries described here are in and around Havana and it's your starting point for a fifth, to Viñales and the tobacco country in the west of the island. You can also set off from here on loops to some of the itineraries to the east: the Zapata Peninsula, Santa Clara and Trinidad – Trinidad is the farthest distant from Havana, more than five hours away by car or bus.

Alternatively, you can weave one or more of these last three itineraries into an overland trip to Santiago, combining it with a stopover in the colonial city of Camagüey (Itinerary 9), which makes an ideal place to break the journey. If going overland, think, too, of stopping at some of the beaches along Cuba's northern coast – such as Cayos Coco and Guillermo (a *cayo* is cay or small, low island) or Guardalavaca.

Providing a counterbalance to Havana in the east of the island – the area known to Cubans as El Oriente – is Santiago de Cuba. Santiago is the country's second city, less than a quarter of the size of the capital with a population under half a million. It's not as cosmopolitan, but it has a distinctive liveliness and some people prefer it to Havana. In addition to being a destination in its own right, it makes an ideal base for trips into the rugged, mountainous areas of the Sierra Maestra and the far east of island, around Baracoa, the last two itineraries of the book.

If you are driving, buy the best map you can find, as signposting is poor.

Note that telephone numbers have all been given their full code: for dialling details *(see page 97)*.

Understanding Street Addresses

Addresses are easy to understand once you know a couple of the shorthands used: C/. = Street (*calle* in Spanish); Ave. = Avenue (*avenida*); e/. or % = between (*entre*); esq. or *esq. a* = on the corner of (*esquina*). In some areas, streets and avenues are named with numbers (as in New York). Hence Calle 3ra. e/. 12 y Malecón is 3rd Street, between 12th Avenue and the Malecón. San Ignacio esq. Muralla is, straightforwardly, on the corners of San Ignacio and Muralla streets.

Left and Right: a fusion of African and Spanish cultures

Havana

1. OLD HAVANA (LA HABANA VIEJA) *(see map, p18–19)*

Old Havana is the historic heart of a fascinating city. It's a mix of the astonishingly well restored and the alarmingly dilapidated: a place to discover by wandering its streets and taking it all in. This full-day's walking tour will show you the key sites of Havana's colonial center. Try to free up at least another day to take in other sites at your leisure.

Starting point: Plaza de Armas, Havana's oldest square.

Havana was founded as San Cristóbal de La Habana in 1515 on the Gulf of Batabanó, on the island's south coast. It was moved to the present site on its splendid bay in 1519 and became Cuba's capital city in 1553.

Make the starting point of your tour Havana's oldest square, the splendid **Plaza de Armas** which, from Wednesday to Saturday, is ringed by antiquarian book stands. In the corner facing the bay is the diminutive but attractive **Castillo de la Real Fuerza** (daily except public holidays, 9.30am–6.30pm; admission fee) built between 1558 and 1577. Once it stored bullion on its way to Spain from Mexico and Peru; now it houses a permanent collection of modern Cuban ceramic art.

Perched on the *castillo*'s highest turret is an aloof bronze figure known as the **Giraldilla** – the symbol of Havana. She is said to be Isabel Bobadilla, the wife of Hernando de Soto, an early Governor of Cuba, and she is searching the horizon waiting for her husband to return from his expedition to conquer Florida. De Soto left Havana in 1539, leaving Isabel to govern Cuba in his place. Four years after his departure she died of grief on hearing he had perished on the banks of the Mississippi.

City Museum and Hemingway Haunt

The 17th-century original Giraldilla, designed as a weather vane, was toppled during a hurricane and can be seen in the **Palacio de los Capitanes Generales** across the square. The Palacio houses the City Museum, the **Museo de la Ciudad** (9am–6.30pm; English-speaking guides available; admission fee), which is arranged around a magisterial, double-tiered courtyard. It has a varied collection ranging from artifacts from

Above: Castillo de Real Fuerza

the independence struggle to enormous shell-shaped marble bathtubs fit to bathe Boticelli's *Venus*. It is worth taking a guide so that you can enter all the rooms. In the upstairs reception rooms hang portraits of plump colonial Captain Generals squeezed into stately breeches, and there is a red damask throne room, prepared for visiting Spanish monarchs – though none showed up.

Leaving the museum, turn up Calle Obispo, passing Havana's oldest house at No 119 (now an antiquarian bookstore) and the **Hotel Ambos Mundos** at No 153, where Hemingway used to stay. You can visit his room, No 511 (10am–5pm; admission fee), which is furnished as it was when he began writing *For Whom the Bell Tolls*. You can also poke your head into two period pharmacies along Calle Obispo: the Farmacia Taquechel at No 155 and Droguería Johnson, No 260, on the corner of Aguiar.

Cathedral Square

Turn right at any of the next streets you fancy, and head back down the parallel Calle O'Reilly to the **Plaza de la Catedral**, perhaps the most beautiful square in the whole of the Americas and as a consequence often filled with tour groups. The imposing facade of the **Catedral de la Inmaculada Concepción** (opening hours vary, but in principle they should be Mon–Tues 1.30pm–5pm, Wed–Fri 10.30am–2pm, Sat 10.30am–2pm, Sun 9am–noon; Mass Sun 10.30am; Mon, Tues, Thur, Fri 7.15am and 8.15pm) was built in the style of a baroque altar. Though

Top: Plaza de Armas
Above: courtyard of the Palacio de los Capitanes Generales

the architecture is characterized more by its width than its height, there's more life to the space inside than you might expect – the unadorned limestone, hewn from an ancient reef, has a fabulous texture, with imprints of fossilized coral and warm, pinkish tints. An elegant octagonal dome rises over the transept. Havana gained its first bishop in 1792.

Stop just around the corner at Empedrado 207 for a creole lunch at the **Bodeguita del Medio**, an atmospheric eatery and drinking hole, where Ernest Hemingway liked to down his *mojitos* (tel: 07-867-1374; noon–midnight; bar till 2am). If the Bodeguita is too crowded for your liking, try the restaurant in the Hostal del Tejadillo, a block away on the corner of Tejadillo and San Ignacio streets.

Boutiques and Restaurants

After lunch, head down one block to the seafront, to browse among the *artesanía* stands at the **Feria de la Catedral** (Tacón e/. Empedrado y Chacón; Wed–Sat 9am–6pm). Then turn back along Calle Cuba or San Ignacio to Calle Obrapía, where you can drop in to the **Casa de la Obra Pía** at No 158, e/. San Ignacio y Mercaderes (Tues–Sat 9.30am–4.30pm, Sun 9.30am–12.30pm; donations), built in 1648 by Don Martín Calvo de la Puerta and continued by his son. *Obra pía* is Spanish for 'pious work' and refers to the charitable foundation set up by Don Martín for five poor orphaned girls, who were given 1,000 pesos a year until they married or joined a religious order.

Turn right at Calle Oficios and walk down to the wonderful **Plaza** and **Antigua Iglesia de San Francisco** (9.30am–6.30pm daily; admission fee) where a *trompe-l'oeil* apse is painted to represent the original, blown down in a cyclone in 1846. It is worth summoning the energy to climb the 42-m (138-ft) high tower, which has one of the best views of La Habana Vieja.

Above: Plaza de la Catedral

Head up Calle Brasil to the **Plaza Vieja**, with its collection of boutiques, tourist-oriented restaurants, bars and the elegant **Casa de los Condes de Jaruco** at Calle Muralla 107 (Tues–Sat 8.30am–4.30pm). This building, dating to 1740, has a splendid patio drenched in climbing vines and some wonderful *vitrales* – the colorful, semicircular windows typical of Cuba in general and Havana in particular – in the upstairs gallery. Contemporary artwork is for sale. Much of the restoration of Old Havana has been made possible through similar enterprises, raising funds for the restoration of Havana while giving local artists the opportunity to display their artwork in suitable surroundings.

Fabulous Churches

One block west is Calle Cuba, which we'll head down to see some more of Havana's most famous religious buildings. First, go into the 17th-century **Convento de Santa Clara** (Mon–Fri 8.30am–5pm; admission fee), which houses a specialist art restoration school. Its cloister – the country's largest – is full of exuberant vegetation, including the *yagruma*, known as the Tree of Hypocrisy because the top sides of its hand-like leaves are a different color from the undersides. The cloister surrounds one of Havana's oldest public fountains, the Fuente de la Samaritana, which was cut off from public use once the convent was built.

Next poke your head into the beautiful **Iglesia del Espíritu Santo**, built in the 1670s for free Blacks and one of the oldest churches in the country to survive intact. A block-and-a-half farther along the route is the **Iglesia de Nuestra Señora de la Merced** (Our Lady of Mercy; Calle Cuba 806; daily 8am–noon, 3–5pm; Mass at 9am daily, Sun also noon), whose Virgin de las Mercedes is linked for devotees of Santería with the *orisha* (guardian spirit) Obatalá, goddess of peace, purity and wisdom. Walk through the scalloped main arch of its restrained, peachy-pink exterior and be surprised by the extravagantly frescoed baroque interior.

Many of the Cubans you see visiting the church will be dressed head-to-toe in white – the color associated with Obatalá. The best day to visit is September 24, the Saint's day, but on the

Right: the cathedral at night

24th of every month the Virgin is paraded around the church during a 6pm candlelit Mass.

One other nearby church is worth a visit, the beautiful **Antigua Iglesia San Francisco de Paula** (8.30am–6.30pm; admission fee), just round the corner. It dates from 1668 and has a collection of modern religious paintings and an impressive stained glass window. You may be lucky enough to catch a rehearsal of the baroque ensemble Ars Longa, which tends to be here in the morning rather than the afternoon.

Music and Mojitos

Return to the Plaza Vieja for a well-earned evening beer in the Cervecería Taberna de La Muralla, where they brew Austrian-style beer in their own micro-brewery; or at the Café Taberna at Mercaderes esq Teniente Rey, decorated in 1950s style, where they play the music of one of Cuba's greatest musicians, the late Beny Moré. Later, when the crowds have thinned, head back to the Plaza de la Catedral for a meal on the romantic balcony of El Patio in the former mansion of the Marquises of Aguas Claras (reserve in advance; tel: [07] 867-1034) and a night spent sipping *mojitos* and dancing below.

Other Highlights

Old Havana merits more than just a day. It has a wealth of interesting museums and if you can spare more time it is well worth visiting some

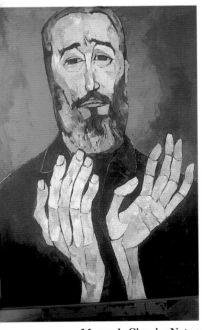

of these. In particular, try to get to the **Museo de los Autos** (Oficios y Justiz; daily 9–7pm; admission fee) whose superb collection of historic cars includes the peppermint-green Oldsmobile that belonged to the revolutionary young-blood Camilo Cienfuegos; the **Casa de Oswaldo Guayasamín** (Calle Obra Pía 111 e/. Mercaderes y Oficios; Tues–Sat 9–4.30pm, Sun 9am–noon; donations), where one of Latin America's greatest artists, the Ecuadorian, Oswaldo Guayasamín, used to paint; the **Casa Natal de José Martí** (Leonor Pérez 314 e/. Egido y Picota; Tues–Sat 9am–5pm, Sun 9am–1pm; admission charge), the birthplace of the great Cuban nationalist hero *(see page 13)*, containing letters, first editions, mementoes, and other items pertaining to his life; and the **Casa de Africa** (Calle Obrapía, 157 e/San Ignacio y Mercaderes; Tues–Sat 9am–5pm, Sun 9am–1pm; admission fee), offering interesting insights into Cuba's African heritage, including Afro-Cuban religions. If you want to see exhibits on Cuba's wildlife you could visit the **Museo de Ciencias Naturales** (Plaza de Armas; Tues–Sat 9.30am–5pm, Sun 10am–3.30pm; admission fee).

Above: Guayasamín's portrait of Fidel Castro in the Casa de Oswaldo Guayasamín

2. CENTRAL HAVANA (CENTRO HABANA) *(see map, p18–19)*

To the west of the city's colonial core is Central Havana, which grew up outside the now-demolished city walls. For this day's tour we'll be skirting the edges of the town on foot to see the most interesting sites. If you have more time, wander into the heart of Centro Habana. It's much safer than its dilapidated *barrio* appearance might suggest, and you get a sense of its energy and what life is like for hundreds of *habanero* families.

Starting point: the Capitolio.

Begin the day with a quick visit to the **Capitolio** building (8.30am–8pm; admission fee). Built in the late 1920s, it acted as the seat of the Cuban legislature until the end of the 1950s, and now houses the Cuban Academy of Sciences. Stop to admire the wonderful bronze portals with bas-relief panels of key moments in Cuban history – look for the defaced heads of the US Ambassador of the early 1930s and the dictator Machado, filed off in the riots that deposed him. Inside the grand entrance hall is a 17m-tall (55 ft) bronze Athena, the Statue of the Republic, and a 24-carat diamond set into the floor, marking the point from where all distances in Cuba are measured. It's a replica; the original Kimberley stone is now in the vault of the National Bank. The colonnaded cafetería here, overlooking the park, is a great place for a coffee.

Cigar Factory Visit

Head round the back of the building to the **Fábrica Partagás**, one of Havana's main cigar factories, ideally in time for the first tour at 9.30am (Mon–Sat, tours every 15 mins, 9.30–11am, 12.30–3pm; no photos; admission fee). Sadly, your $10 entrance fee doesn't buy the opportunity to see cigars being rolled on the thighs of virgins – it's a myth – but the reality is fascinating nevertheless. You'll see all the stages, from selection of the leaf to quality control and packaging the final product in Cana-

Above: the Capitolio
Right: Fábrica Partagás

dian cedar-wood boxes. Some 250 rollers (*torcedores*) turn out 25,000 cigars a day here, while a reader reads to them from a lectern: early in the morning it's *Granma*, the official newspaper; followed by romances or detective stories chosen by the workers. Quotas vary depending on the type of cigar and, although their pay is linked to productivity, a good roller will still earn in a month only what you paid for your 45-minute tour.

Head next to the **Parque Central** to see some of Havana's most notable 19th- and 20th-century buildings, including the **Gran Teatro** and the **Hotel Inglaterra**. Crossing the square, you'll find El Floridita (11am–midnight), where one of the world's classic cocktails was perfected. By this time of day, Ernest 'Papa' Hemingway would have already worked his way through 11 frozen double *daiquirís*, unsweetened. Either they were considerably less expensive than now or his books were selling well, but you may baulk at the $6 price tag. Still, you might like to see the bronze statue of Papa adopting his favorite pose. Loop by the Art Deco **Edificio Bacardí** and the **Hotel Plaza** up to the tree-lined Paseo de Martí, known as the **Prado**. Promenade, as 19th-century high-society would have done, down this fabulous boulevard to Calle Trocadero, past one of Havana's most famous hotels, the Moorish-influenced **Sevilla**, where Al Capone, Josephine Baker and Jim Wormold (Graham Greene's *Man in Havana*) once stayed. On Sundays, the Prado is the scene for an informal art market with a mixed bag on display.

The Major Art Museums

Either side of lunch, visit two major, but vastly different museums. The first is the **Arte Cubano** section of the **Museo Nacional de Bellas Artes** (Fine Arts Museum), at Trocadero e/. Zulueta y Monserrate, a three-story modernist building that houses the premier art collection in Cuba. You can easily spend a couple of hours here; start at the top and work downward. The powerhouse of the collection is the work of 20th-century Cuban artists, but it has strong colonial and contemporary sections, too. There are works

by Eduardo Abela (1889–1965), including *Guajiros* painted in 1938, depicting a group of men in white sombreros preparing for a cockfight; Fidelio Ponce de León (1895–1949), whose haunted, wasted figures have echoes of El Greco; René Portocarrero; and Wilfredo Lam (1902–82), Cuba's Picasso. Look out for the Afro-

Left: Eduardo Abela's *Guajiros* in the Museo Nacional de Bellas Artes (above)
Right: buildings on the Malecón

havana

Cuban influences in Lam's abstract art – you'll almost always see the presence of the *orisha* Eleguá – the guardian of houses. Here, too, is the thickly textured oil painting, *La Silla* (1943), perhaps the second most famous chair in art, after that painted by Van Gogh.

Memories of the Revolution

Return to the Sevilla for lunch and a swim ($10 for use of the pool, but that includes $8 of drinks or snacks). If it's Sunday you might want to take a quick look at the outside of the second museum, the Museo de la Revolución *(see below)* on Calle Refugio before hopping in a taxi to Callejón Hamel for Afro-Cuban dancing and music (Sunday only; noon–3pm). The murals on Callejón Hamel are the project of Salvador, a self-taught artist whose work is found from Venezuela to New York and Norway and whose studio is on this street.

On other days, there's more time to spend at the **Museo de la Revolución** (10am–5pm; English-speaking guides; admission fee), housed in the former Presidential Palace of the dictator Batista. In the glass building in the square between the Fine Arts museum and the Palace you can see the *Granma*, the boat that brought Castro from Mexico to start the Revolution in 1956 *(see page 14)*, and the turbine of a U2 spy plane, shot down on October 27, 1962, at the height of the Cuban Missile Crisis. The neoclassical palace was built in 1913, and served as Presidential Palace from 1920 until 1965. In 1957 it was stormed by some 50 students hoping to assassinate Batista. Although some got as far as his private office, he escaped through a secret passage, which you can see. Half the students were killed in the attack.

Upstairs is a much-photographed mock-up of Camilo Cienfuegos and Che Guevara in guerrilla pose, along with personal possessions of these two dead heroes of the Revolution. English translations in the museum make it possible for non-Spanish speakers to learn all about the official view of the Revolution from the 1950s to the present day.

Back on the Prado, wander along to the **Castillo de San Salvador de la Punta**, part of Havana's old defenses; and then stroll up Havana's renowned seaside boulevard, the **Malecón**, as far as the Monumento Antonio Maceo – at its best in the evening. For an evening meal, try Doña Blanquita's on the Prado, or choose a spot in **Chinatown**.

3. VEDADO *(see map, p18–19)*

Vedado is Havana's main business district, with high-rise hotels and government buildings. It's spread out over a large area, so for this day's tour of the main sights, you'll need to combine legwork with the occasional taxi.

Starting point: Plaza de la Revolución.

A revolutionary start to the day, beginning at the immense expanse of the **Plaza de la Revolución**, a square that's seen political speeches, military parades and gatherings of up to a million people. Surveying all these proceedings is a giant image of **Che Guevara**, taken from Albert Korda's iconic photo and bolted into the facade of the Ministry of Interior. Spread across the other side of the square is the **Palacio de la Revolución**, nerve centre of

the State, where the Central Committee of the Communist Party, the Council of State and the Council of Ministers meet. Dominating everything, at the center of the square, stands the **Memorial José Martí** (Mon–Sat 9am–5pm, closed Sun; English-speaking guides; admission fee) – an enormous marble obelisk, at the foot of which is a statue of the poet and Cuban National Hero. José Martí (1853–95) has left an indelible stamp on Cuban history, not merely due to the fruits of that prominent forehead, but also due to an energy belied by his slight physique. He is best known abroad for his *Versos Sencillos* (*Simple Verses*; first published in 1891), which were later set to music in the song *Guantanamera*; but to Cubans of all political persuasions, be they right-wing Miami exiles or extreme *Fidelistas*, he is the epitome of the Cuban patriot. He warned presciently against the dangers of US expansionism and was martyred for the Cuban cause in 1895 at the outset of the war he helped to start, the Second War of Independence.

It's worth paying the extra US$2 to head up to the top of the 109-m (358-ft) high tower. The tallest point in Havana, it affords unparalleled views.

Tales from Beyond the Grave

Take a local *Coco Taxi* (a small motorcycle with a canopy on the back) to the **Cementerio de Colón**, whose monumental main gate is at Zapata s/n y Calle 12 (9am–5pm; English-speaking guides; admission fee). Among the eclectic mausoleums of Cuban notables is one to a woman known simply as La Milagrosa for her supposed miracle-working powers. Her real name was Amelia Goyri, and she was buried with her baby when both died during childbirth. Some 13 years later, when her husband came to bury his father, he lifted the lid of her coffin and found that Amelia's body

Above: Ministry of the Interior building, Plaza de la Revolución

hadn't decayed, and the child that had been buried at her feet was now in her arms. Women come to seek her intercession to help fertility, and there's a collection of ex-votos left in thanks.

Juana Martín, a passionate domino player, thought she had one particularly tense game sewn up, and had a heart attack when her opponent snatched an unexpected victory. Her gravestone is a double-three – the domino she had left in her hand as she prepared for victory.

Pre-Columbian Finds

Have lunch in one of the cafés across from the main gate. Then hop into a taxi and head for the University of Havana, with its anthropological museum, the **Museo Antropológico Montané**, on the upstairs floor of the Felipe Poey building (Mon–Fri 9am–noon and 1pm–4pm; admission fee). This is the finest collection of Pre-Columbian Cuban artifacts. Pride of place goes to the Idol of Tobacco: made of guayacán wood in about AD900, it has shell eyes, a headband and a carved phallus. There is little evidence to link it with a tobacco god: other theories suggest it was a funerary urn or a god of war; but traces of hallucinogens inside indicate it may have been an elaborate ceremonial mortar. Nearby is an amazing collection of Napoleonic memorabilia, the **Museo Napoleónico**, in the Florentine-style villa at San Miguel 1159 esq Ronda (Mon–Sat 9am–4.30pm; admission fee). The 7,000 items were amassed by a 19th-century Cuban landowner, Julio Lobo, and include a cast of the death mask that Napoleon's doctor made in St Helena, two days after his death.

From the Napoleonic era to the space age, we move on to the **Coppelia**, at the corner of La Rampa and Avenida L (11am–10.30pm), for a lunchtime ice cream. This curious structure looks like something out of *Close Encounters of the Third Kind* crash-landed among the Copey fig trees and palms. Inside you'll be ushered to a communal table in one

Above: the memorial to José Martí
Right Coppelia ice cream is delicious

of six circular satellite rooms – pay 5 Cuban pesos (US$0.20) for an *ensalada* of mixed ice cream. The 1990s film *Fresa y Chocolate (Strawberries and Chocolate)* took its name from here. These are still often the only flavors on the menu. Inside it's not always the rich Coppelia brand of ice cream being served, but you can always track this down at the stands on the edge of the park: it's seriously delicious and US$1.50 a scoop.

Mafia Hangout

If it's a Sunday, you might like to dance off this indulgence by heading to **Callejón Hamel** *(see page 29)* for Afro-Cuban dancing and music. Otherwise, head along La Rampa to the historic **Hotel Nacional**, Cuba's most famous hotel. It was inaugurated in 1930, and soon became a favorite for Hollywood stars and Mafiosi: there were times in the 1940s when the whole hotel would be taken over by Mafia clans for interfamily 'conferences.' Its heyday was the 1950s, when the likes of Marlon Brando and Spencer Tracy came to stay. The bar has an exhaustive gallery of celebrities on the wall, listing everyone from Jiang Zemin to the Back Street Boys. One unusual feature of the landscaped hotel garden is the anti-aircraft defenses, constructed during the 1962 Cuban Missile Crisis.

If you still have energy, head down to the **Monument to the Victims of the Maine** on the Malecón, dedicated to the 260 American sailors who died in 1898 when their ship exploded in the Bay of Havana. It triggered US intervention in the Cuban-Spanish war, with all its later consequences. In fact, it's likely the sinking was caused not by a Spanish torpedo, but by an explosion in the hold.

You may also like to visit Vedado's artisans' market, the **Feria del Malecón** *(see page 73)*, which is a short taxi ride away.

For an evening meal, try one of the many restaurants in the Hotel Nacional, or there's a *paladar (see page 75)*, Los Amigos, which serves hearty *criollo* food (Avenida M, e/. 19 y 21, Vedado; tel: (07) 830-0880), open till midnight. Arrive early or there'll be a line, as it's popular with local *habaneros*. Otherwise, you could head out to Marianao for a meal and a night's cabaret at Havana's world-famous Tropicana *(see page 79)*.

4. AROUND HAVANA *(see map below)*

A day's tour to the eastern part of the city and outlying spots, including Hemingway's home, starting at the historic port of Regla and covering around 40km (25 miles).

Starting point: The ferry for Regla leaves regularly (6.15am–10.15pm) from opposite the end of Calle Santa Clara, costs $0.10 moneda nacional *and takes 10–15 minutes. To prevent the boat being hijacked and taken to Miami, there's a control point, and no knives or glass bottles are allowed. If using a rental car, take a good map and head for Regla on the Avenida del Puerto/Primer Anillo del Puerto from Habana Vieja, not via the tunnel to El Morro.*

Step off the ferry at **Regla** and visit the restrained 17th-century **Iglesia de Nuestra Señora de Regla** (Mon noon–5.30pm, Tues–Sun 7.30am–5.30pm), dedicated to the Virgin of Regla, the Patron of Havana. Dressed in baby blue, the dark Madonna holds a white baby Jesus and occupies pride of place in the baroque altar. For Santería believers, she represents the *orisha* Yemayá, goddess of maternity and the sea. The Virgin's day is September 8, but a good time to visit is the 8th of any month when they parade her on the patio at 10am.

A couple of blocks inland at Calle Martí 158 is the **Museo de**

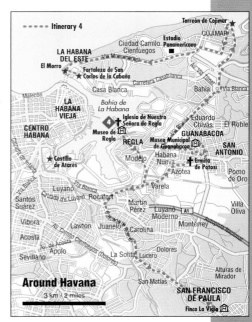

Regla (Tues, Thur–Sat 9am–6pm, Wed 1–9pm, Sun 9am–1pm, closed Mon; admission fee). This documents the vibrant history of the port that saw huge influxes of slaves, auctioned as they came off the ships, and the arrival of the first Chinese laborers in the mid-19th century. About this time, too, Regla became the first site where the Afro-Cuban religion of Abakuá took hold; and the first *cabildos* (groups of mutual assistance) were founded here by Babalao Remigio Herrera, a prince from the Lukumí ethnic group who was brought here as a teenage slave. You can see Herrera's Eleguá – the Santería *orisha* who guards the believer's house – along with an expanding collection of Afro-Cuban religious artifacts.

Hemingway's Home

From here, it's a taxi ride (ask the museum staff to call one if there are none around) to the southern suburb of San Francisco de Paula and the former home of Ernest Hemingway, **Finca La Vigía**, now a museum (Calle Vijía s/n Km 12.5, Calzada de Güines; 9am–4.30pm, closed Tues; admission fee). Hemingway's third wife, Martha Gelhorn, came across the house in 1939 and thought it a good move – Hemingway was receiving far too many visitors in the Hotel Ambos Mundos, to the detriment of his writing. They ended up buying the house for $18,500 at the end of 1940, using

Top: garden of the Finca La Vigía
Left: just as Hemingway left it

part of the $150,000 film rights to *For Whom the Bell Tolls*. Here he wrote *The Old Man and the Sea*, *Death in the Afternoon* and *Islands in the Stream*. Hemingway lived here until July 1960. A year later, in the throes of a depression, he blew his brains out in Idaho. His fourth wife, Mary Wells, left the house and its contents – including some 9,000 books and first editions of nearly all his books – to the Cuban state, according to his last wishes.

His house has been kept just as it was when he died: the armchair bar with his half-drunk bottles of Campari, Bacardi and Havana Club; the trophies from safari hunts; shelves groaning under the weight of books; a miniature cannon he would fire to salute the arrival of special guests; the Royal typewriter on which he wrote his 500–600 words-a-day. In the gardens is the pool where actress Ava Gardner once swam naked, and his yacht, the *Pilar*.

Afro-Cuban Religions

Take a taxi back in the direction of Regla and on to another historic town with Afro-Cuban connections, **Guanabacoa**. At Calle Martí 108, e/. Versalles y San Antonio, you'll find the **Museo Municipal de Guanabacoa** (Tues–Sat

10am–6pm, Sun 9am–1pm; admission fee) in an attractive 19th-century colonial mansion. This is famous for its collection of items linked with the syncretic Afro-Cuban religions – Santería, Abakuá and Palo Monte. One room has been set up to show how an initiate or follower of Santería would have his home, and you'll see that the *orishas* are very much part of the family. In Santería, the *orisha* chooses the believer, not the other way round, offering his or her protection; and the exhibits include a *canastillero* – the display cupboard where all the offerings and *orishas* are kept.

Farther on, look for the *egué*, the sacred drum of Abakuá, hidden behind a veil, as it shouldn't really be exhibited. Guanabacoa is one of the few places in the country where Abakuá is practised: it's a religion that admits only men, and is based around secret societies where members swear mutual assistance, regardless of the consequences. Its complex rituals involve elaborate drumming and dance.

There are also exhibits related to Palo Monte, which has similarities with Santería, but whose roots lie in the Bantú cultures of Angola and the Congo. It is linked with the worship of spirits and natural, elemental forces. *Paleros* (believers) make offerings and communicate with the spirits via a *Nganga*, an iron cauldron that contains key elements, including a piece of human bone. Magic symbols are also used for divination.

Las Orishas restaurant, just along the street from the museum, is a good option for a late lunch. Otherwise, Hemingway fans should take a taxi to the

Right: Santería altar, in Regla, a center of Afro-Cuban religions

fishing village of **Cojímar** – the place that inspired *The Old Man and the Sea*. You can have lunch at La Terraza (Calle Real esq. Candelaria; 10.30am–11pm; set lunch costs $12), a crestfallen little restaurant overlooking the bay. The bay, called La Boca, is past its prime, but in the far corner are the marlin- and shark-fishing boats the community uses, and old photos on La Terraza's wall depicts the hut where the original Old Man lived. A couple of blocks away is a mini castle, the **Torreón de Cojímar**; and next to this you'll find the small cast bust of Hemingway that the local fishermen had made out of scrap metal.

Then it's back along the coast toward Havana to visit **El Morro** (or El Castillo de los Tres Reyes Magos del Morro; daily 8am–8pm; admission fee), Havana's sentinel fortress and a UNESCO World Heritage site. There's a great view from the top of El Morro's lighthouse, Cuba's oldest. The beam reaches 33km (18 nautical miles) out to sea. It was built between 1589 and 1630 by the Italian, Giovanni Battista Antonelli (Juan Bautista to the Spanish). A great chain used to run from here to the Castillito de La Punta on the far side, which would be lowered to let ships pass. The only time it succumbed to enemies was in 1762 when Anglo-American forces besieged El Morro and went on to capture Havana. Now El Morro houses three museums, the best of which charts the history of the voyages of discovery and displays a reconstruction of an indigenous *caney* dwelling.

For an evening meal with a great view across the harbor towards Habana Vieja, head to La Divina Pastora at the foot of the neighboring San Carlos Fortress (tel: 07-860-8341; noon–11pm), where they serve high-quality seafood. If the view is less important than the cost, opt for Hostal Doña Carmela opposite the entrance to the Fortaleza de San Carlos.

Aim to be inside the sprawling **Fortaleza de San Carlos de la Cabaña** (daily 10am–9.30pm; admission fee), often known simply as La Cabaña, by 8pm, in time to wander round and then see soldiers in ceremonial livery light the touch paper for **El Cañonazo**, the 9pm one-gun salute. This ceremony once signaled the closure of the city gates. The fortress was built after 1763 following the English occupation of Havana, and is the largest built by the Spanish in the Americas. The bills were so huge that the King of Spain at the time, Carlos III, asked for a telescope to be brought to him – at 14 million pesos, he felt it had to be large enough to be visible from Madrid.

Western **Cuba**

5. VALLE DE VIÑALES AND TOBACCO COUNTRY *(see map, p38–39)*

The heart of this tour is a two-day, 410km (255 mile) round-trip by car from Havana that visits one of the island's most photogenic tourist destinations, the Viñales Valley, for an overnight stop. Time permitting, give yourself three to five days so you can take advantage of some interesting add-on options: one or two of Cuba's finest beaches – María La Gorda (240km/150 miles) and the one on the island of Cayo Levisa (3km/2 miles long) – and a national park.

Starting point: take the autopista *west of Havana toward Pinar del Río.*

Day one is fast paced. Leave Havana early (ideally before 9am) and head past Pinar del Río and on toward the rich brown soils of **Vuelta Abajo**, a triangle of land that lies broadly between the settlements of San Juan y Martínez, San Luis and El Corojo. It's here that the finest tobacco leaves in the world are grown, and we're heading for the area of Las Cuchillas de Barbacoa, to **Las Vegas de Robaina** (tel: 08-797470; Mon–Sat 10am–5pm, closed Sun; English-speaking guide; tours last one hour; admission charge). These are the fields *(vegas)* of perhaps the best tobacco-grower in the world. What Compay Segundo was to Cuban music, Sr Alejandro Robaina is to Cuban cigars. A gentleman well into his eighties, with a face as distinguished as one of his finest dry leaves, he's a real ambassador, traveling the world to promote the country's prestigious product. He is the only living person with a brand of Cuban cigars named after him, and this is the only plantation that is authorised for tourist visits. There's a mystique here that you don't find in the tobacco factories – the smells, the sounds, the breeze, the pampered wrapper leaves growing under a fine gauze to protect them from the sun's scorching rays. It's the perfect place to learn all about the painstaking processes, from planting through to hand-rolling the final *habano puro*.

Finding Las Vegas de Robaina is a challenge: there are plenty of touts in the area who will offer to take you to it, then take you somewhere entirely different. Heading south from Pinar, turn left after 13km (8 miles) at the first main turn-off, in the direction of San Luis. Some 4km (2½ miles) down this road turn left down a dirt road, and then it's first left, first right, first right and the house is on your left, about 1.5km (1 mile) from the San Luis road. If you're unsure, just ask for the *casa de Señor Robaina*.

Left: the World Heritage site of El Morro
Right: Sr Alejandro Robaina among his crop

From here, if you've opted for the longer version of this itinerary, continue down to the diving resort of **María La Gorda** and the excellent nature destination of **Península de Guanahacabibes** and its **national park** (*see page 69*). Rejoin the itinerary a day or two later in Viñales. Otherwise, head straight back through Pinar del Río and on to the scenic delights of the **Valle de Viñales**.

Classic View

As you approach the Valley, take the detour left to the **Hotel Jazmines** for one of the classic views of Cuba, a carpet of small farms and thatched tobacco-drying barns spread out over the fertile red soil of the land below, and out of this flat-bottomed valley floor thrust the steep-sided *mogotes* (residual limestone hills) of the Sierra de los Órganos. The hump-backed *mogotes*, covered by a unique type of forest, are reminiscent of the Guilin karst hills of China, and are all that remains of giant collapsed caves. It all seems slightly unreal.

Not half as unreal, however, as the bizarre **Mural de la Prehistoria** (8am–9pm; admission fee), a colossal mural painted on the side of one of the Dos Hermanas *mogotes*. To get there head into the little town of **Viñales**, turn left at the first main T-junction, going back out of town, and then turn right 2km (1¼ miles) farther on. Love it or hate it, the mural is decidedly

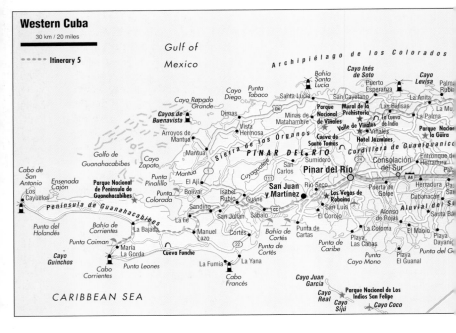

whacky, a post-revolutionary project that depicts life forms from this area, from ammonites and plesiosaurs through to Guanahatabey indigenous people. The restaurant here is a favorite with coach tours, but for once it's understandable. They serve some of the very best meat you'll taste in Cuba – the charcoal-roasted pork melts in your mouth.

You may now want to head back into Viñales, a friendly, languid place that spreads out along its main drag, Calle Salvador Cisneros.

In the afternoon, try to take advantage of the beautiful countryside with a bicycle or horseback ride, or a guided walk through this unique environment, or by visiting the home of a *guajiro* farmer. The hotels organize trips or you can ask at your *casa particular*. If you're starting in Viñales, you might like to consider a trip out to a semi-flooded cave full of stalactites, **La Cueva del Indio** (Apr–Oct 9am–5.30pm, Nov–Mar 9am–5pm; admission fee), 8km (5 miles) to the north of town. The cave is rather overpriced and the half-hour guided tour is a hit-and-miss affair, but the boat trip through the flooded section is fun.

In the evening, head to Viñales's oldest building, Casa de Don Tomás, at Salvador Cisneros 140 (10am–10pm). Here you can sit out on the veranda and tuck in to the house specialty, *Las Delicias de Don Tomás*, a paella-like dish of yellow rice with meat and seafood, washed down with a pineapple-and-rum El Trapiche cocktail.

Botanical Garden and Biosphere Reserve

Next day, if you're heading to **Cayo Levisa** *(see page 69)*, you'll need to leave Viñales for 8.30am to reach **Palma Rubia** in good time for the 10am ferry (check ferry times in Viñales). Palma Rubia lies 3km (2 miles) off the main coastal road; the turn-off is signposted, some 9km (6 miles) east of the Manuel Sanguily intersection. An early-morning (9am) boat back the next day or the day after will give you plenty of time to reach the Sierra del Rosario for late morning and lunch.

If you're not visiting Cayo Levisa, then there's no rush. Have breakfast first and then enjoy a brief trip to the **botanical garden** of the sisters Caridad and Carmen Miranda (donations), on the left as you drive out of town to the north, at Salvador Cisneros 5. There's no science here, just an infectious love of plants, and one of their volunteers will show you around the huge variety of exotic fruit trees in the chaotic backyard. Then

Left: Mural de la Prehistoria near Viñales

head north and west along the coast road toward Bahía Honda. This goes through undulating scenery, past sugar cane fields and stands of royal palms. Flanking the route on the right is the Cordillera de Guaniguanico, the range that runs down the entire western flank of Cuba and includes the Sierra de los Organos and the next mountains along the route, **La Reserva de la Biosfera Sierra del Rosario**, which now form a UNESCO biosphere reserve. Take the unsignposted road 6km (4 miles) east of Bahía Honda through San Diego de Núñez, from where the road rises into the thickly wooded mountains. After some 17km (10 miles), branch off left toward Las Terrazas, passing through the control point (admission fee).

The eco-community of **Las Terrazas**, 11km (7 miles) from the junction, is an unusual and interesting place. The collection of rather dated, low concrete buildings overlooking an artificial lake is built on solid principles of sustainable development, and there's an obvious and genuine sense of community among the thousand or so residents. Inaugurated in the late 1960s, it was designed to bring together *campesinos* from all over this region and provide them with improved housing and basic services. There's an excellent hotel, Hotel Moka *(see page 93)*. You can always head back to Havana early next morning – it's only an hour or so away.

Ask at the Hotel Moka about riding a horse or walking to the Baños del San Juan, 4km (3 miles) away, where there's a natural swimming hole. It's also fun poking around some of the little workshops in the community – there are a number of artists' studios, and the locals produce quality, original crafts, from carvings to handmade paper.

You have two fabulous possibilities for lunch. The first is in the community itself: El Romero, a truly rare thing in Cuba – a high-quality vegetarian restaurant (tel: 082-778555, 778625; 9am–9pm). They take pride in what they do, serving a variety of healthy dishes and anti-stress juices using local organic and wild produce. Alternatively, leave Las Terrazas and turn right at the main road. Immediately before the exit from the reserve,

turn left up a narrow track – the staff on the control gate need to radio ahead to check no cars are coming down. At the top of the 2km (1 mile) track is the **Cafetal Buena Vista** (tel: 082-778555 for reservations; 8am–5pm), a beautifully restored, stone-built coffee *finca* dating from 1802. Lunch, for US$13, is a tasty *criollo* meal, usually of oven-roasted chicken, which you can enjoy while taking in the views.

Above: view across the valley, Viñales
Left: bulls of Viñales

Central **Cuba**

6. ZAPATA PENINSULA AND THE BAY OF PIGS *(see pull-out map)*

This is a one- to two-day 126km (78 mile) tour, including birdwatching or fishing in Cuba's most famous wetland nature reserve, the Zapata Swamp, and a trip to the site of the failed 1961 Bay of Pigs invasion.

From Havana take the autopista *southeast of Havana toward Santa Clara.*

A bit of forward planning will enable you to make the most of your time. Reserve your guides a day or two in advance: you'll save a few dollars by doing this direct with the National Parks office – EMA – in Playa Larga (tel: 0145- 97249); or call the Information Center (tel: 0145-93224) next to the Rumbos restaurant on the Havana to Santa Clara highway at the main Jagüey Grande/Zapata intersection. This Information Center can also arrange fishing trips ($130–250 per person per day): the area has some world-class sport fishing for bonefish *(macabí)*, tarpon *(sábalo)*, snook *(robalo)* and barracuda *(picuda)*, but you'll need to bring your own kit as there's none to rent.

If you're to take advantage of the birding or fishing tours, it's best to stay in the Bohío Don Pedro *(see Accommodations, page 93)*, as the timings of the boats to and from Hotel Guamá don't let you take advantage of dusk or dawn. If nature's not your thing, you can hit the sites you don't need a guide for – La Boca, Guamá, the *cenote* and Playa Girón – from Havana.

Swamps, Lagoons and Woodland

The Zapata Peninsula covers 3,300 sq km (1,275 sq miles) of flatlands and was declared a UNESCO biosphere reserve in 2000. It's described as a swamp, but it has several different habitats and only small sections are permanently under water. There are expanses of sawgrass dotted with palms; mangrove-fringed lagoons; a few rivers and flooded drainage canals; dry evergreen woodland; and semi-deciduous woodland. Eighteen of Cuba's 22 endemics are among 230 species of birds seen here, and there are 12 species of mammals, including *jutías* (a type of rodent) and iguanas.

Nature tours last up to four hours, and there are several options, costing $10–15 per person. You will need your own transportation, either a rental car or a taxi, and your own binoculars. For a good overview of the different types of habitat to be found on the peninsula, you will need to take around three tours.

Right: Cuba is a paradise for anglers

Take a boat trip along the **Río Hatiguanico**, which is much more atmospheric and 'swampy' than one to Guamá *(see below)*. Organize this to link with your journey to or from Havana, as you access the river from a motorway turn-off, 40 minutes west from the main Jagüey Grande crossroads. A morning trip is best, as this will give you an opportunity to see two rare endemic species: the Zapata wren *(ferminia)* and Zapata sparrow *(cabrerito de la ciénaga)*.

A trip to **Bermejas** – ideally also in the morning, the next day – will take you into dry, seasonally flooded woodland, where you can see such Cuban specialties as the smallest bird in the world, the bee hummingbird *(zunzuncito)*; the almost equally tiny, delightful Cuban tody *(cartacuba)*; the national bird, the Cuban trogon *(tocororo)*; the Cuban green woodpecker *(carpintero verde)*; and the Cuban pygmy owl *(sijú platanero)*.

Finally, a trip to **Las Salinas** is great for viewing such salt-flat waders

as flamingos, roseate spoonbills *(sevilla)* and many species of heron.

The Cuban Crocodile

Following an early morning nature tour, visit **La Boca** crocodile farm (daily 9am–6.30pm; admission fee), 8km (5 miles) past the control gate, where you can learn about the endangered, endemic Cuban crocodile. They'll show you how to lasso one of these beasts. The Cuban crocodile can be distinguished from its American cousin by its longer, finer snout, the ridges on its head, and smaller spots. Though shorter, it is squatter, heavier and more aggressive. Although some crocs are raised for releasing back into the wild, 80–90 percent fall prey to the jaws of tourists in La Boca's restaurant (open for lunch, till 4.30pm).

If you're not packing in morning and evening nature tours, take a boat trip from La Boca to the reconstructed Taíno village and hotel complex of **Guamá** (allow 1½ hours to make the round trip; $10 per person). Boats leave every 15–30 minutes (9am–6pm) down a long, straight drainage canal frequented by ospreys to the **Laguna del Tesoro**, a great expanse of browny-green waters fringed by low swamp vegetation. Legend has it that the lake holds in its depths a great treasure, thrown there at the time of the Conquest by the Taíno to hide it from the Spanish. Maybe the 'mermaids' in the lake know something about it: a handful of introduced manatees – the creature that inspired the mermaid myth – survive in the lake, although you'd be lucky if you actually saw one. On the far side of the lake is Guamá, named after a *cacique* (chief) who rebelled against the Spanish in Baracoa in the 16th century. Here you'll find the Taíno village, populated by a rather listless group of Cubans paid to dress up as natives, and a series of highly romanticized sculptures of the Taíno as the noble savage. The hotel itself makes a great place to stay out of the wet season, if you're not keen on doing nature tours *(see page 93)*.

Above: La Boca crocodile farm

central cuba

The Bay of Pigs

Head south, past Playa Larga and along the shores of the **Bahía de Cochinos** (the Bay of Pigs) to Playa Girón. The Bay of Pigs was probably named by sailors who came here to provision their boats with wild swine. Eighteen kilometers (11 miles) past Playa Larga is the **Cueva de los Peces** (The Fish Cave; daily 8am–6pm; admission fee), a beautiful example of a Caribbean *cenote* sinkhole, ringed by dry woodland. This aquamarine *cenote* is about 70m (230ft) deep and is inhabited by more than a dozen species of saltwater fish, including parrot fish and wrasse, although these disappear into the depths if you dive in. The best time to visit is late morning, when the sun lights up the waters. The restaurant makes a much more pleasant lunch stop than La Boca, although the food is plain and the portions are small.

Next stop is the **Museo Girón** at Playa Girón (8am–noon, 1–5pm; admission fee), which chronicles the dramatic events of the ill-fated US-sponsored invasion of April 17–19, 1961. Outside is a British Sea Fury airplane used by the Cubans to repel the invaders, along with replicas of the defenders' Soviet-made tanks. Inside are newspaper cuttings and black-and-white photos of the Cuban 'martyrs' – 156 combatants and five civilians, along with some of their shirts, belts and berets that have bullet holes and faded bloodstains.

Even if you don't speak any Spanish it's worth paying the extra dollar to see the 15-minute video of propaganda news footage from the time. As PR disasters go, the US couldn't have done much worse, and Castro reveled in reminding the world that this marked 'the first defeat of Yankee Imperialism in the Americas.' Two hundred 'mercenaries' were killed and 1,197 taken prisoner, to be tried in public courts that demonstrated 'their miserable moral condition.'

Above: coastline, the Bay of Pigs
Right: British Sea Fury, Museo Girón

7. TRINIDAD *(see map below)*

Two nights (1½–2 days) in and around one of Latin America's most beautiful colonial jewels – a town of cobblestone streets and brightly painted houses, built on sugar wealth. It has been protected since the 1950s, and has been on UNESCO's list of World Heritage sites since 1988.

Starting point: Trinidad is 290km (180 miles) southeast of Havana.

Trinidad was the third of Diego Velázquez's seven villages. It was founded in 1514 at a site near Cienfuegos but moved to an indigenous settlement on its present site when gold was discovered. The town had a shaky start. First the gold ran out. Then, following Hernán Cortés's departure from here in 1519 to conquer the Aztec Empire, settlers left to seek their fortune in Mexico. Gradually, the town started to develop an economy based on cattle farming, smuggling and small-scale tobacco and sugar cultivation. Pirates and corsairs raided in the 17th century.

However, it was white gold – sugar – that brought the boom years to Trinidad from the end of the 18th to the mid-19th century. First the trade in slaves was liberalized, providing a workforce. Secondly, the slave revolution in Haiti in 1791 caused planters to flee and sugar production there to collapse. Trinidad received this wave of immigrants and set about supplying the market as Haiti had done once. Suddenly Trinidad became an economic powerhouse and one of Cuba's wealthiest towns: between 1766 and 1846 there was an 11-fold increase in sugar production, and the new *sacarocracia* (sugaristocracy) built lavish mansions filled with European luxuries. By 1851, 14,000 slaves were toiling in the fertile Valle de los Ingenios.

Growing abolitionism, the wars of independence and increased competition from European sugar beet helped pitch the industry into a subsequent steep decline and Trinidad slipped once more into provincial obscurity.

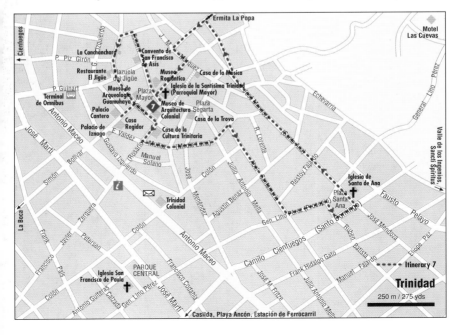

The Historic Center

Begin your time in Trinidad with a day's gentle moseying tour of the pedestrianized historical center. The natural place to start is the **Plaza Mayor**, full of appealing details such as the imported glazed urns and bronze greyhounds, and overlooked by the **Iglesia de la Santísima Trinidad**, also known as the Parroquial Mayor. To the right of the church as you face it is the Escalinata, a staircase where the town's slave auctions used to take place. To the left, at Fernando Hernández Echerri 52, is the **Palacio Brunet**, a beautifully proportioned colonial mansion that contains the **Museo Romántico** (Tues–Sun 9am–5pm; admission fee). The first floor of the house dates from 1740, the upper story was added later, and it takes its name from a count, the Conde de Casa Brunet, who inherited it through marriage in 1830. Most of its collection of furniture was donated by Trinitarian families, and you get an idea of the eclecticism of the *sacarocracia* – finely carved Cuban hardwood chairs, a Marie-Thérèse enameled writing desk, blue Venetian crystal, and some gorgeous cedar cabinets.

From here, wander along the cobblestone streets to the **Convento de San Francisco de Asís**, with its shapely bell tower, one of the most photographed buildings in Cuba. Inside the Convent is the **Museo de la Lucha Contra Bandidos** (Tues–Sun 9am–5pm; admission fee), detailing efforts to root out those who fought against Castro's Revolution in the Sierra del Escambray in the 1960s, but you can give this a miss and just climb the tower. Next, go down past one of the town's oldest buildings, the 18th-century **La Canchánchara**, named after a drink that used to put fire in the bellies of the 19th-century independence fighters, the *mambises*. A mix of rum-like *aguardiente*, lime and honey, it's served here in terra cotta cups.

Pass through the **Plazuela del Jigüe**, where Bartolomé de Las Casas *(see page 11)* conducted the area's first Mass in 1513 when this was still an indigenous settlement, known to the Spanish as Manzanilla. The Restaurante del Jigüe here is a good place to return to later for a Creole lunch (Calle Rubén Villena esq Piro Guinart; tel: 01419-4315).

Keep walking toward the Plaza Mayor to visit the **Museo de Arqueología Guamuhaya**; 9am–5pm, closed Fri; admission fee). Exhibits chronicle the presence in the area of indigenous peoples, Africans

Above: Iglesia de la Santísima Trinidad
Right: Palacio Cantero

and Spanish. The building also houses the **Museo de Ciencias Naturales Humboldt**, named after the German scientist, naturalist and outspoken opponent of slavery, who dined here in 1801 on a brief stopover in Trinidad. It is interesting to speculate on the dinner table conversation that may have taken place between Humboldt and his slave-owning hosts.

Artisans' Street Stands

One of the joys of Trinidad is just wandering its streets, appreciating little characteristics such as the graceful iron window grilles *(rejas)*. To tap into this, cross town to the **Plaza Santa Ana**, going via Calle Ernesto Valdez Muñoz (known, as with most streets in Trinidad, by its old name, Media Luna). This street and some of its offshoots are lined by artisans' stands – the linen on sale is a Trinitarian tradition. Stop in the Plaza Santa Ana to see its eponymous, ruined church. Then head back via Calle José Mendoza (Santana) and climb the hill to another tumbledown church, the Ermita Nuestra Señora de la Candelaria de la Popa – **La Popa** for short – for a wonderful view of the town.

Return to the center to see the Casa de Aldemán Ortiz, where you'll find *artesanía* and artwork for sale. In the late afternoon, visit the **Palacio Cantero**, home to the **Museo Histórico Municipal**, (9am–5pm, closed Fri; admission fee). Its high-ceilinged rooms have been opulently furnished in the style of a 19th-century sugar baron's mansion. Exhibits are dedicated to slavery and the sugar industry, including a 1.2m (4ft) high bronze bell that tolled to signal working hours, a fire or the escape of a slave at one of the nearby plantations of the powerful Iznaga family. Best of all, though, is to climb the

wooden steps to the top of the square tower and soak up the view, ideally in the late afternoon light, of Trinidad on the curve of the Sierra del Escambray, as it drops down toward the coast and the beach hotels at Playa Ancón.

For an evening meal, head to the Sol y Son *paladar* (small homely restaurant) at Simón Bolívar 283, e/. Frank País y José Martí. Then, at night, visit Trinidad's main street where you'll find three lively nightspots: choose from traditional music at the Casa de la Trova (Fernando Echerri 29, e/. Jesús Menéndez y Patricio Lumba; 9am–1am, with a show starting at 9pm; admission fee); an

Above: Trinidad's characteristic *rejas*
Left: 'La Popa'. **Right:** street scene

central cuba

Afro-Cuban folkloric show at the Palenque de los Congos Reales (9pm–2am, with the show starting at 10pm; admission fee) half a block away toward the Plaza Mayor; or varied entertainment under the stars at the Casa de la Música, at the top of the Escalinata, round the corner.

Steam Train to a Sugar Estate

The next morning, take the **Tren Turístico** steam train trip to the **Valle de los Ingenios** to visit the historical, UNESCO-protected sugar estates (train leaves 9.30am daily; $10 round trip). It's great fun: arrange a taxi to pick you up at Manaca-Iznaga *(see below)*, which allows time for one of the afternoon options recommended below (ask the driver to be there for 11.30am; $10 approx; 13km/8 miles by road). If you're a train buff, you can do the whole round trip to Guacinango (where you can swim in the shallow Río Ay), in which case you should be back in Trinidad for about 3pm.

The US-built locomotive dates to 1907. With much whistling and puffing, it trundles out of town and down into the cane fields of the valley below on the 20km (12-mile) trip to the terra cotta-roofed hamlet of Manaca-Iznaga, taking 45mins to an hour. Here you visit the **Hacienda de Iznaga** (7am–5pm), a well-appointed colonial *hacienda* that was one of the many around here owned by one of Trinidad's most powerful sugar-growing families. Run the gauntlet of vendors selling lace to climb the octagonal 43.5m (142 ft) tower, the **Torre Manaca-Iznaga** (9am–5pm; admission fee), built in 1820 as a lookout to spot escaping slaves. From the top, it affords views across the valley toward the forested **Sierra del Escambray** mountain range, with the Topes de Collantes peak cresting like a green wave in its midst.

It'll probably be too early to try the *criollo* food on offer at the Hacienda, but you might like a drink. In its back garden there's an original **sugar press** (*trapiche*), where they sell sugar cane juice (*guarapo*) for US$1 – you can buy it for a lot less by the train tracks.

If you have an extra half-day to spare, choose one of two options. The fit and energetic might visit the **Topes de Collantes** resort (tel: 0142-540219, 540117; comercial@topescom.co.cu), on the other side of Trinidad, where there's a challenging walk to the dramatic, 75m (244ft) Salto Caburní waterfall (3hrs; $6.50 per person; guide obligatory – reserve ideally a day in advance). If it's leisure you're seeking, head to the beach at **Playa Ancón**, a 12km (8 mile) taxi ride away.

8. SANTA CLARA AND REMEDIOS *(see pull-out map)*

This is an easy-paced day tour, which combines a dose of Revolutionary history in the town of Che Guevara with a relaxing afternoon moseying around a small provincial backwater with sufficient colonial heritage to make it a national monument. Depending on where you plan to travel next, you can return to Santa Clara for the night, stay in Remedios, or continue to the beach at Cayo Santa María.

Starting point: Santa Clara is on the autopista, *275km (170 miles) east of Havana.*

The town of **Santa Clara** seems irrevocably linked with the fate of one man: Ernesto 'Che' Guevara, the Argentine-born doctor and icon of the Revolution. All Cubans, it seems, claim him as one of their own, but for the residents, it's more clear-cut than that – he's a *santaclareño*. It was here that Guevara won the battle that secured the Revolution's victory in 1958;

and it is here that his bones have found their final resting place, after having lain – handless – for 30 years in a common grave in Bolivia, where he was executed.

Che Guevara Remembered

There's no escaping Guevara, so dive in: take a taxi or drive to the enormous statue of Che – part of the **Conjunto Escultórico Ernesto Che Guevara** – that overlooks the Plaza de la Revolucíon, 2km (1 mile) to the west of the town center. Beneath this monument is his **mausoleum** (Tues–Sat 8am–9pm, Sun 8am–5pm; bags and cameras must be handed in at the cloakroom), an emotionally charged place designed as a guerrilla cave. When his bones were brought here in 1997, more than 100,000 turned out to pay their respects; but Che is not buried alone. He is accompanied by other comrades who fell during his Bolivia campaign: sculpted faces of Bolivians, Cubans, Peruvians and one Argentinian woman peer out of their niches in the suppressed light. They are labeled with their combat names, and there are no dates of death – they're supposed to be resting here, ready to restart the struggle at any time. Even the eternal flame has been designed to evoke a campfire, burning to keep them warm.

Changing the scene, head to the town's focal point, **Parque Vidal**, where there's always plenty of life. It's a good place to grab a coffee and – facing away from the anomalous, pistachio-green Hotel Santa Clara Libre – enjoy the architecture. Look in on the beautiful **Museo de Artes Decorativas** (Mon, Tues, Thur 9am–noon, 1–6pm, Fri & Sat 1–6pm, 7–10pm, Sun 6–10pm; admission fee) to see its eclectic collection of period furnishings.

Above: statue of Che Guevara overlooking the Plaza de la Revolucíon
Top Right: the Museo de Artes Decorativas. **Right:** *coche* transport, Santa Clara

Then head out in the direction of Remedios. On the outskirts of town, 1km (½ mile) from the square, park up to see the **Monumento al Tren Blindado** (Mon–Sat 8am–6pm, Sun 8am–noon; admission fee), commemorating the events of December 29, 1958. At this strategic moment in the struggle, Che and 17 of his men succeeded in derailing this armored train and, armed only with rifles and Molotov cocktails, managed to capture more than 400 of Batista's reinforcements, along with cannon, bazookas, rocket-launchers and machine guns that they were taking from Havana to use against the rebels in the east of the island. The victory proved decisive. Che's forces went on to capture Santa Clara, severing Batista's communications with the Oriente. Days later, Batista fled to Santo Domingo in exile.

Provincial Life in Remedios

Leave town by the same road, heading for one of Cuba's oldest towns, **Remedios**, a small place of crumbling, low colonial buildings. The town was burnt down once in 1578 by French pirates; and again in 1691 in a fratricidal struggle with Santa Clarans who were trying, in vain, to get the townspeople to relocate.

Despite its history, Remedios has few places to visit but it is attractive in a low-key way and gives a real feel of provincial Cuban life. You can hang out on the main square, Plaza Martí, watching people meandering around on their bicycles, or just wander the back streets.

Sites include the town's main church, the **Templo Parroquial de San Juan Bautista**, on the corner as you enter Plaza Martí. Inside, a remarkable Churrigueresque gold-leaf altar rears out of the gloom, contrasting with the solid whitewashed walls, while above is a polychrome *mudéjar* ceiling made of cedar. Founded in 1550, the church owes much of its look to the wealth and passion of one 20th-century millionaire, who bartered and bought much

of what you see, to create the only totally baroque interior in all Cuba. Even the magnificent altar, which looks so at ease with itself, was not built as one piece – the millionaire bought a chunk of it from a church in Bejucal, but only by promising to restore what was left of that church, too.

Looking diagonally across the plaza you'll see another venerable church, the **Iglesia del Buen Viaje** (closed for restoration).

Famous Street Festivals

Although generally a sleepy place, Remedios sparks into action for its Christmas *parranda* street festivals, which you can learn about in its best museum, the **Museo de las Parrandas** (Tues–Sat 9am–noon; 1–6pm, Sun 9am–1pm; admission fee), a block-and-a-half off the square down Calle Máximo Gómez *(see Calendar of Events, page 82)*.

Even out of the festive season, nights can be surprisingly lively around the main square. El Louvre (pronounced *loo-vray*; Máximo Gómez 122) has an open-air terrace perfect for people-watching. Founded in 1866, it's the longest continuously functioning café in Cuba and it exudes charm, but sadly only serves snacks (open till 2am). Alternatively, try the Restaurante Las Arcadas in the adjacent Hotel Mascotte – it's indoors, but has good service and a better selection of food (open till 10pm).

9. CAMAGÜEY *(see map, p52)*

A day wandering around a laid-back, untouristy provincial capital, set in the heart of Cuba's cattle country.

Starting point: midway across the island, 485km (300 miles) southeast of Havana, Camagüey is a natural stopping-off point if traveling the length of the island overland.

Camagüey has a rich tradition of art and music; but is most famous for its colorful colonial and neoclassical architecture, its churches and the large, traditional earthenware jars, called *tinajones*, once used for water storage. Its historical center has been designated a Cuban National Heritage Site. The layout is labyrinthine. It was designed to deter invaders, following attacks by pirates, and many streets are still referred to by their pre-Revolution names.

One of the original seven Cuban towns, Camagüey was founded in 1514 as Santa María del Puerto del Príncipe, near present-day Nuevitas. A chronic lack of water, infertile land and plagues of mosquitos forced the settlers to try another site, before arriving here in 1528. The name of Puerto Príncipe

Above: the gilded altar in the Templo Parroquial de San Juan Bautista, Remedios

stuck until 1903, when it adopted the name of the province, itself originally the name of a *cacique* (chief) in the region at the time of the Conquest.

Make your starting point the central square, **Parque Ignacio Agramonte**, where a fine equestrian statue of the local hero brandishes his sword. Agramonte was one of the five great men of Cuba's wars of independence, an impetuous but charismatic leader who was shot while fighting the Spanish in 1873.

The south of the square is dominated by the cathedral, and on its western side are two noteworthy buildings: the **Casa de la Trova** and, next to it at Calle Cisneros 106, an enchanting blue-and-white art nouveau house from 1906, being converted into a museum of decorative arts.

The People's Hero

Take the street leading out of the southeast corner of the square toward the photogenic **Plaza San Juan de Dios** and its eponymous, recently renovated church, both dating from the early 18th century. Next door is the former church hospital, now the **Museo San Juan de Dios** (Mon–Sat 9am–5pm, Sun 9am–1pm; admission fee) and here, at the back of the cloister, a memorial plaque marks the spot where Agramonte's body was put on display after his death. His legacy to the town is profound: Camagüeyans identify themselves as *Agramontinos* – the only people in Cuba to have taken their patronymic from a revolutionary hero.

Amble back to the main square and then west along Calle Martí to the **Plaza del Carmen**, named after its church, the Iglesia

Above: Plaza del Carmen, Camagüey
Right: Camagüey's bronze statue of Agramonte

Nuestra Señora del Carmen. This cobblestone plaza has been lovingly restored and, aside from the delightful pastel-colored buildings, it's notable for the fun, chocolate-brown *marmolina* statues of *Agramontinos* engaged in daily life, made by Martha Jiménez Pérez. Her nearby studio is open for afternoon visits (General Gómez 274B, e/. Lugareño y Mas Vidal, opposite Callejón del Príncipe; www.pprincipe. cult.cu). Before that, you may like to stop at El Ovejito (tel: 0132-292524) on the square for lunch.

Double back and head along Calle Hermanos Agüero, dropping in for a brief visit to the **Casa Natal Nicolás Guillén** at No 58 (Mon–Fri 8am–4.30pm), the modest birthplace of Cuba's most famous 20th-century poet. Guillén (1902–89) championed the common man and Castro's Revolution, while as a mulatto he identified closely with his Afro-Cuban heritage, spicing his poetry with its rhythm, language and imagery. Some of his works

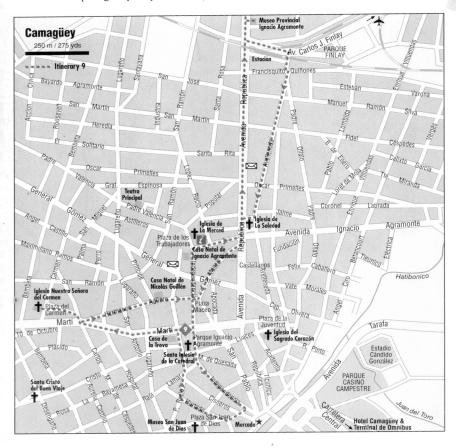

are displayed – in Spanish only – on the walls. The place is brought alive by the young musicians who come here daily to practise.

Turning left at Calle Independencia will bring you to the **Plaza de los Trabajadores** and Agramonte's birthplace, the **Casa Natal Ignacio Agramonte** (Tues–Sat 9am–4.45pm, Sun 8am–noon; admission fee). He came from one of Puerto Príncipe's wealthiest cattle-owning families and trained as a lawyer, as you see from the dashing photo of him with student friends. The building has been restored in period style with displays of Agramonte's personal effects, including his ivory-handled Colt revolver.

Hop on a *bicitaxi* (US$1) to reach the eclectic **Museo Provincial Ignacio Agramonte** at Avenida de los Mártires 2 e/. Ignacio Sánchez y Rotario (Mon–Thur 10am–5pm, Fri 2.30pm–10pm, Sat 10am–5pm; admission fee). Built in the 19th century as a barracks for the Spanish cavalry, it has an excellent collection of furniture, including an extraordinarily grandiose 19th-century display cabinet made for the American, Horacio Rubens, when he was President of the Cuban railroads; and a small but choice collection of Cuban art, including works by the *Agramontino* Fidelio Ponce de León. In the natural history section downstairs, the 19th-century watercolor prints of Caribbean fish are delightful. Tours of the museum are in Spanish only.

Finally, head back to the Parque Agramonte for a drink at the attractive Bar El Cambio, done up with an effective old-time look. Drop in, too, to the Galería Jover next door at Martí 154, the home of the artists Joel Jover and his wife, Ileana Sánchez.

Evening Options

For an evening meal, it's worth braving the rather stuffy atmosphere of the *paladar*, El Cardenal, at Martí 309, e/. Hospital y San Antonio (food served until 11pm). The chicken and pork dishes are huge and tasty. Wash your meal down with a Tínima, the locally brewed beer – the smoother, stronger variety, with a red label is better than the blue.

For entertainment, there are a number of good options. The Casa de la Trova *(see page 51)* has live *son*, *trova* or Afro-Cuban music depending on the night (Tues–Thur 9pm–midnight,Fri–Sun 9pm–2am; it is worth reserving a table in advance). Better still, catch a ballet, a concert or a performance from one of Camagüey's impressive folkloric dance troupes performing at the **Teatro Principal** (Calle Padre Valencia 64, e/. Tata Méndez y Lugareño; tel: 0132-291991 or 293048).

Right: a mural by Ileana Sánchez brightens up a corner of Camagüey

El Oriente

10. SANTIAGO DE CUBA *(see maps, p56)*

A full-day tour of Cuba's second city. If you're thinking of coming in the second half of July, when Santiago erupts into Afro-Cuban *carnaval* mode, you should definitely extend your stay.

Starting point: Plaza de la Revolución. Santiago is 861km (535 miles) from Havana, at the opposite end of the island, and a two-hour flight or a 12-hour drive.

From its foundation in 1515 until 1553 Santiago was the capital of Cuba, and though it has since been eclipsed by Havana as a metropolis, it is a place with a vibrant cultural mix and a proud tradition of music and rebellion. The slogan it proclaims as you drive into the city – *'Rebelde Ayer, Hospitalaria hoy, Heroico Siempre'* ('A Rebel Yesterday, Hospitable Today, Heroic Forever') – sums up the place nicely.

Aim to make an early start and, if you haven't already seen it on your way into the city, begin your tour in the **Plaza de la Revolución**, with its striking socialist-realist equestrian **monument** to one of the great heroes of the wars of independence, the 'Bronze Titan,' Antonio Maceo Grajales. Maceo didn't get his nickname for nothing – this mountain of a man, more than 6ft (1.8m) tall and weighing 120 kg (260lb), fought 800 battles and survived 25 bullet wounds before the 26th killed him, in 1896. The monument's jagged forest of black blades represents the machetes of his *mambís* independence fighters.

Working your way back into town, head to the **Antigua Cuartel Moncada** and the **Museo 26 de Julio** (Tues–Sat 9am–7.30pm, Sun 9am–1pm; admission fee), to learn about Castro's first, abortive attempt at revolution. On July 26, 1953, under cover of *carnaval*, Castro and around a 100 co-conspirators tried to storm these barracks. The assault went disastrously awry and 61 of the young revolutionaries were killed: only six in combat; the rest were tor-

tured and subsequently murdered. The torture was horrific – the eyes of one of the leaders, Abel Santamaría, were plucked out and brought to his sister, a fellow combatant, on a plate. Castro himself escaped a similar fate by a whisker – although he initially escaped to the mountains of Gran Piedra, he was captured days later. But the second-lieutenant who caught him sympathized with the rebels and opted to disobey orders, driving Castro in a non-military truck to a civilian jail where his capture became public knowledge, rather than 'disappearing' him into Moncada.

Homes of the Famous

From Moncada, take a taxi south to the **Casa Natal Antonio Maceo** at Maceo 207, e/. Corona y Rastro (Mon–Sat 9am–5pm; admission fee). Inside this simple, early-19th-century house you'll find personal items and a rather macabre brooch made from the tooth of his mother, the redoubtable Mariana Grajales. As a mulatto, Maceo was prohibited from attending school, but he managed to more than hold his own on an intellectual level among the white elite. He was respected by José Martí and became a great friend of Máximo Gómez.

Head to the town center for a walking tour, beginning at the main square, **Parque Céspedes**, which acts as the beating heart of the city, both day and night. Facing you is the imposing **Catedral de Nuestra Señora de la Asunción**, and opposite is the blue-and-white colonial-syle **Ayuntamiento**, a 1950s reconstruction of the 17th-century town hall. The first thing to visit is the much more modest-looking **Casa de Diego Velázquez** (Sat–Thur 9am–1pm, 2pm–4.30pm, Fri 2pm–4.30pm only; admission charge), believed to be the oldest house in Cuba and home to its founding *conquistador*. Santiago was the last of the seven towns Velázquez and his men established, and this house was built as both his private residence and seat of governance. It remained the official residence of the city's Governors until the mid-18th century, and then went through various uses, becoming little more than a low-rise tenement before restoration started in the 1960s. The house now functions as the **Museo de Ambiente Histórico** – its rooms have been beautifully re-created to show how they would have

Left: Santiago de Cuba. **Above:** Parque Céspedes. **Right:** the cathedral

been furnished in the 16th to the 19th centuries. Enjoy the wonderful *mudéjar* ceiling, much of which has survived intact from the 16th century; and look for the oven that may well have been used for smelting what little gold the *conquistadors* found on the island.

If you're feeling a little peckish, find a table in the first floor café of the Casa Granda hotel on the opposite corner of the square. It's pricey, and the service could be better, but its location is first-rate for watching the comings-and-goings on the square. You can get a bird's-eye view of the square by zipping up in the elevator to the 5th-floor bar.

The Museum that Rum Built

Next wander up bustling **Calle Heredia**, with its artisans' stands, passing the Casa de la Trova *(see page 58)*; and the **Casa Natal J.M. Heredia**, birthplace of one of Cuba's greatest 19th-century nationalist poets (Tues–Sat 9am–8pm, Sun 9am–2pm; admission fee). Turn left at Pío Rosado for half a block to find the grand neoclassical **Museo Bacardí** at Pío Rosado (Carnicería) s/n, e/. Aguilera y Heredia (Mon noon–9pm, Tues–Sat 9am–9pm, Sun 9am–1pm; admission fee). The country's first museum, and one of its best, was founded in 1899 by Emilio Bacardí, the son of the founder of the rum dynasty and a great patriot during the wars of independence. Hugely respected

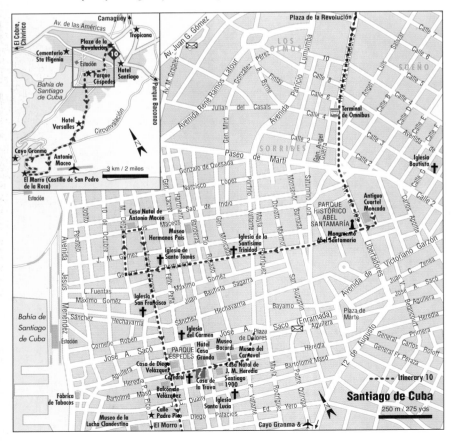

both in his time and since, he became Santiago's first mayor on independence, and was a renowned philanthropist. This eclectic museum has torture devices from the time of the Spanish Conquest; a huge assembly of artifacts linked to the wars of independence, including a coffin-shaped *Mambís* torpedo, the saddle Antonio Maceo was using on the day of his death and his enormous leather gaiters; some idiosyncratic forays into ancient history; and an excellent, wide-ranging collection of Cuban art. Finely executed portraits include the watery-eyed alcoholic Negro by the Santiagan artist José Joaquín Tejada Revilla (1867–1943); a raffish pipe-smoking self- portrait by Juan Emilio Hernández Giro (1882–1953); and the square-jawed, pugilistic *El Galeno* by Joaquín Cuadras (1843–75).

Return to Heredia where, on the corner at No. 303, is the **Museo del Carnaval** (Tues–Sun 9am–5pm; admission fee). The country's most famous carnival takes place between July 21 and 27, with a parade, *conga* celebrations, fireworks and all-night partying. This museum charts the festival's origins. Santiago has a well-deserved reputation for its fiery music and dance, and you can get a flavor of this most days at 4pm here, when a group of musicians brings the place to life by pounding out Afro-Cuban rhythms on their *batá* drums in the patio at the back. Ask at the museum how to track down one of the city's main *conjuntos folklóricos* (folkloric ensembles) – Cutumba, Folklórico Oriente, La Caridad de Oriente or 19 de Setiembre *(see pages 81–82).*

Fabulous Fortress

Wander up Heredia to the attractive **Plaza de Dolores** to have a drink in one of the cafés and then take a late afternoon 7.5-km (4-mile) trip by taxi to the beautiful, 17th-century **El Morro** fortress (9am–7pm; admission fee), a UNESCO World Heritage Site. The Castillo de San Pedro de la Roca, to give it its full name, commands fantastic views of the coast, the tight entrance to the bay, and back toward the city. It is hard to envisage a more commanding position. The English privateer Henry Morgan said he could defend the bay from here with one dog and a rifle. Construction started in 1638, to the designs of Juan Bautista Antonelli, the son of the man who designed Havana's El Morro, and its great arrow-shaped terraces took 70 years to build. Inside are exhibits on the history of piracy, including a rogue's gallery of pirates, buccaneers and corsairs.

The Morro is an excellent place to watch the sunset when the *cañonazo* is fired (5.30–6.40pm, depending on the time of year). Unlike at the more famous ceremony in San Carlos fortress in Havana, the people who light the touchpaper here aren't dressed in the costumes of Spanish colonial soldiers, but of *Mambís* independence fighters.

Right: El Morro, Santiago de Cuba

Dine in the El Morro restaurant next door (9am–9pm; tel: 0122-691576). It serves *criollo* food and has a fine view from the terrace. Then it's back into Santiago city for a night of song at the **Casa de la Trova** on Calle Heredia (11am–1am; admission fee). Santiago has music flowing through its veins, and this spot pays homage to masterful Cuban musicians of the past, some of whom were regulars here. It's now highly organized, pitched primarily at tourists, but still delivering feisty music and a great atmosphere. Eliades Ochoa, the Grammy-award-winning exponent of *guajira* music, makes regular appearances.

Excursions from Santiago

For those with slightly longer in the city, two other half-day excursions are well worth taking. The first is to **Gran Piedra**, a 1,234-m (4,050ft) peak to the east, and its neighboring coffee farm, **La Isabelica** (8am–4pm; admission fee). The second, if you're not planning on doing the Sierra Maestra loop, is a trip to the **Basílica de Nuestra Señora de la Caridad del Cobre** *(see page 63)*.

11. THE SIERRA MAESTRA ROUND TRIP *(see map, p62–63)*

This adventurous three- to five-day trip by rental car around the Sierra Maestra mountain range covers 621km (386 miles) and visits some of the most resonant sites of both the struggles for independence and Castro's Revolution. Although a four-wheel-drive is not absolutely necessary, it helps in places – the dramatic coast road can be affected by landslips, the sea washes gravel and sand on to some stretches, and the gradients around Villa Santo Domingo are extreme.

Starting point: Santiago de Cuba.

The time you spend on this tour depends on what hiking options you take from Santo Domingo. You can do the round trip in three fairly fast-paced days if you're just interested in visiting Comandancia de La Plata: spend night one in Niquero; night two in Santo Domingo; and get up early on day three to do the walk. Doing the loop in four days gives you either a second night in Santo Domingo (you'd do the same walk, but the rest of the day is just for hanging out) or a night

in Bayamo; and either way you should be back in Santiago for mid-afternoon on day four. Five days allow you to climb Pico Turquino as well as visit the Comandancia: spend nights two and four in Santo Domingo, and night three in a refuge on the climb (bring your own sleeping bag and food). Guides are obligatory on all hikes: call the Flora y Fauna headquarters a day or two in advance to reserve one who speaks English (*un guía que habla inglés*;

Left: the coast below the Sierra Maestra

7am–6pm; tel: 0123- 565349). For all options, day one involves getting some distance under your belt: aim for Marea del Portillo or Niquero.

Rugged Coastal Route

On the way out of Santiago visit the city's **Cementerio de Santa Ifigenia** (Calle Raúl Perozo s/n; 8am–6pm; admission fee), which is a *Who's Who* of deceased Cubans. Pride of place goes to the **Mausoleo de José Martí**, the tomb of Cuba's great hero. The place is suffused with light, as Martí didn't want to be buried in the dark like a traitor. Other famous people buried nearby include Carlos Manuel de Céspedes, the Father of the Homeland about whom we'll be learning more in the tour.

Ask directions and head out west, skirting the foot of the Sierra Maestra range, toward Chivirico. Stop for a leisurely lunch at the Sierra Mar, a large resort hotel about 12km (8 miles) before Chivirico – $10 gives you an hour's access to their buffet, pool and beach (it's $3/hr after that).

Past Chivirico the mountains come closer to the sea: Cuba's highest peak, **Pico Turquino** (1,974m/6,476ft), rears up from the rest of the range, although its summit is frequently shrouded in cloud. The next stretch of highway, especially after Las Cuevas, is the most rugged and magnificent of the coastal route. If you like beaches, **Marea del Portillo** is the place to stay on night one – it's not one of Cuba's classics, but is still pleasant: a wide arc of grayish-white sand encircling the calm waters of the bay. Alternatively, you can press on, leaving the main mountains behind and turning inland at Pilón to **Niquero**, a scruffy but lively place on the Guacanayabo Gulf. Dominated by its enormous sugar mill, Niquero comes alive on Saturday and Sunday nights when the townsfolk wheel out El Mulato del Oriente – a street organ that wheezes out a range of stomping punch-card tunes. Dancing and drinking rum, the whole town seems to come out on the streets to pay homage to El Mulato.

The Most Southerly Point

On day two, head southwest, past Niquero, to the **Parque Nacional Desembarco del Granma** (A UNESCO Natural World Heritage Site; admission fee). The park protects a valuable coastal habitat, and was established around

Above: Niqueró's sugar mill at dawn

the spot south of Playa Las Coloradas where Castro and some 80 revolutionaries landed in December 1956, after a nightmarish seven-day trip from Mexico. A replica of the *Granma* stands on the side of the road.

Some 10km (6 miles) farther on is what is Cuba's most southerly accessible point, **Cabo Cruz**, where there's an attractive 19th-century **lighthouse** and a half-forgotten fishing village. Drive carefully, as the great undulations in the road hide some nasty potholes.

Double back past Niquero, heading past **Media Luna**, home town of the revolutionary Celia Sánchez. Farther north, 4km (2 miles) beyond Calixito, you reach the turn-off to the **La Demajagua** estate (7am–5pm; admission fee), where, on October 10, 1868, Carlos Manuel de Céspedes famously rang the liberty bell, freeing his slaves and raising the cry of 'Independence or Death' to start the First War of Independence. It's a peaceful spot overlooking the sea; and the monument is tastefully designed, incorporating the remains of Céspedes' sugar mill, which was bombed to smithereens a week later by a Spanish naval ship, in reprisal. The port of **Manzanillo** makes a good lunch stop. Head into the center of town and amble round the attractive main square, with its Moorish bandstand. If it's not too busy, try El Golfo on the silty bay, at Primero de Mayo y N. López (tel: 0123-53158) for a great-value seafood lunch, charged in Cuban pesos. Service is slow on busy weekends, when you might like to try another peso restaurant, Las Américas, at esq. Maceo y Martí on the plaza.

From Manzanillo head inland again, as far as **Yara**, where in all probability the *cacique* Hatuey was burned alive *(see page 11)*. It was also here that Carlos Manuel de Céspedes, who had left La Demajagua after proclaiming revolt in 1868, first encountered Spanish troops and suffered a crushing defeat. His gesture of defiance became known as the 'Grito de Yara' – the Cry of Yara.

A Hike into the Sierra Maestra

At Yara, take the turning south toward **Villa Santo Domingo**, passing rice paddies and sugar cane on the way to Bartolomé Masó, and then climbing up into the Sierra Maestra. The hotel Villa Santo Domingo is the base for treks into the wonderful, densely forested **Parque Nacional de Turquino**, and you can contract the obligatory guides at the information center just past it. The hikes start from **Alto del Naranjo**, 4km (2 miles) away, up an extreme gradient of 40 percent in some places. Underpowered or overloaded cars will not make it, so if your car is not up to it, you'll have a 90-minute walk.

To get a real flavor of what it must have been like for Castro and his band of guerrillas during their revolutionary campaign, walk to their mountain headquarters, the **Comandancia de la Plata** ($11 per person with a guide). It's about an hour's walk from Alto del Naranjo (reckon on at least three hours round trip). Though pretty much anyone can make it, there are ups-and-downs and it's often muddy, so bring decent footwear and water. No photos are allowed in the camp: Fidel reputedly believes anyone who wants to see the camp should have to put in some legwork – as the rebels did. Not so much his legwork, however, as that of the eight people who lugged the vast, kerosene-powered refrigerator for 30km (18 miles) up to the cabin. Though strafed with bullets from one of Batista's planes, the fridge is still in full working order.

You can visit the Comandancia and climb the **Pico Turquino** ($33 per person extra; 13km/8 miles each way from Alto del Naranjo) in two whole days, but aim to leave early on day one. Included in the price is a night's stay at the Aguada Joaquín refuge, where there are sheets, mattresses and drinking water; but bring water for day one, all your own food, suncream, a hat, warm rainproof clothing and a sleeping bag, as it can get cold. The hike involves stiff climbs, but the forests are marvelous and – when the clouds aren't down – you're rewarded by amazing views down to the coast below.

Heroic Independence Town

Some two hours' drive from Santo Domingo is patriotic **Bayamo**, the capital of Granma Province, and a town proud of its feisty, independent his-

Top Left: the liberty bell, Demajagua. **Left:** Moorish bandstand in Manzanillo.
Above: Bayamo mural. **Over Page:** Nuestra Señora de la Caridad del Cobre.

tory. The town was founded at a site on the Río Yara in 1513 as the second of Diego Velázquez's seven communities, and it was moved here the following year. It has a history of contraband and struggles with pirates, but is most famous for the crucial role it played in the First War of Independence.

Following his defeat at Yara, Carlos Manuel de Céspedes was left with only 11 men, but they went on to take strategic but poorly defended Bayamo, assisted by a population sympathetic to the cause. On the day the city fell, October 20, 1868, the words of what was to become the National Anthem were sung for the first time, and a provisional government declared. The country's first 'free' government was multiracial, but did not include women. Céspedes signed the decree abolishing slavery here in December that year, but the nascent republic soon ran into problems. The city, with no natural defenses, is difficult to defend, and when in 1869 Spanish troops closed in, the citizens decided to torch their town rather than hand it over. The conflagration lasted three days, consuming 90 percent of the town.

Reminders of the city's past are everywhere: a statue of Carlos Manuel de Céspedes stands in Napoleonic pose in the main square, the **Parque Central**, also known as Parque Céspedes. Look for the defiant words ('*Oscar no es mi único hijo...*') that he sent to the Spanish Capitán General Caballero de Rodas in 1870. The Spanish had captured his oldest son, threatening to execute him if Céspedes didn't renounce his views. Céspedes famously wrote back 'Oscar is not my only son. I am the father of all Cubans who

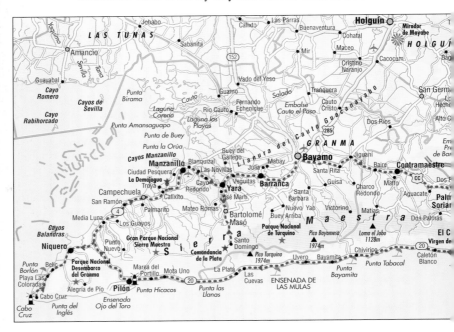

have died for the Revolution…' – words that led to him being called the Father of the Homeland. Oscar was shot by firing squad.

Fronting the Parque at Maceo 57 is the **Casa Natal Carlos Manuel de Céspedes** (Tues–Fri 9am–5pm, Sat 9am–2pm, 8pm–10pm, Sun 10am–1pm; admission fee), his birthplace and one of the few buildings that survived the great fire of 1869. Here you can see the letter Céspedes sent to Caballero de Rodas and trace the life-story of this multitalented man.

A block from the main square, on the cobbled **Plaza del Himno Nacional**, is the **Catedral San Salvador** (9am–noon, 3pm–5pm). The current building dates to 1919, although there has been a church on this spot since 1514 when its priest was Bartolomé de Las Casas *(see page 11)*. Inside the cathedral is a dramatic canvas depicting the moment in 1868 when, surrounded by *mambises*, the local priest blessed Céspedes' new Cuban flag. The painter, Julio Sangles, is the bald gentleman looking at you from the far left-hand side.

For a good-value lunch, try the *paladar* El Polinesio, Parada 125 e/. Pío Rosado y Capotico (noon–10pm) some four blocks from the Parque Central.

Home of the Goddess of Love

Returning to Santiago, make your final stop the **Basílica de Nuestra Señora de la Caridad del Cobre**, the holiest shrine in Cuba (6.30am–6pm) 15km (9 miles) to the northwest of Santiago in the foothills of the Sierra Maestra. The basilica is home to Cuba's patron saint, the **Virgen del Cobre**, a black Madonna who, for Santería believers, represents Ochún, the goddess of sweet waters, love, fertility and sensuality. Legend has it that the statue of the Virgin was discovered when it came to the rescue of three fishermen who were caught in a storm in the Bay of Nipe. She now occupies the apse behind the altar where you'll also find a remarkable collection of ex-votos. There's a steady flow of pilgrims to the basilica, peaking on her saint's day, September 8.

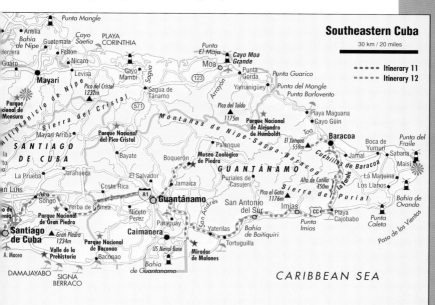

12. EAST TO BARACOA *(see map, p62–3)*

A two- to three-day 305-km (190-mile) trip from Santiago to the country's oldest city, Baracoa. If you don't mind driving long distances, an option is to head north via Moa, toward Guardalavaca *(see page 69)*, or to loop back round to Santiago. Don't, however, try the tempting route marked on many maps via Palenque – the road conditions are extremely rough and it's a prohibited military zone (you are liable to be arrested). A visit to look out over Guantánamo naval base must be arranged in advance with a tour agency in Santiago – vouchers cost about $5 per person. You must arrive at the military checkpoint between 10am and 2pm (last entrance). Visit takes 1hr–1½hr. You will be escorted by the Administrator from the checkpoint to Malones and can eat at the restaurant there.

Starting point: Santiago, but the trip to Baracoa can also be made in reverse. So as not to duplicate a 300-km (190-mile) drive, the trip is best done by combining a flight with an overland journey by taxi or rental car, although you'll be charged a fee for not returning the car. If you're short of time, drop the overland section and fly in and out of Baracoa.

It's about 1½hr from Santiago to the city of **Guantánamo** – as you come into the latter's northern fringes, don't head for the city center, but ask for the *camino a Jamaica* and head towards the village of Boquerón. Your first stop is the **Museo Zoológico de Piedra** (7am–6pm; admission fee), a quirky sculpture park near Boquerón, and a favorite off-beat tourist site. As it's a tourist

site *(sitio turístico)*, you *are* allowed to visit, though you may need to remind the police gently about this at the checkpoint before Boquerón. You're not allowed beyond the museum – the mountains of Guantánamo province are a military zone.

The sculpture park is a fantasy grove, a stone menagerie under the banana palms, mangos and orange-flowering *búcaro* trees. All the animals have been carved by Angel Iñigo Blancodehenaia and his son, Angelito Iñigo Pérez. Señor Angel began carving the limestone boulders on his land on a whim in 1977, using his imagination and what he'd gleaned from books and TV, and there are now more than 400 carvings, from turkeys with their chicks to a full-size baby elephant. Allow 1½hrs for this 24km (15-mile) detour.

Head back towards the city of Guantánamo, but again, avoid the city and turn east towards Baracoa. Some 22km (13 miles) past the main traffic circle is the turn-off and checkpoint for **Mirador de Malones**. Arriving with your ticket between 10am and 2pm, you will see a remarkable slice of Cold War history, which you can digest over lunch. Guantánamo – or Gitmo to US servicemen – is the US's oldest overseas military base. Although sovereignty lies with Cuba, the US lease is indefinite and can only be voided if the US abandons the area or through mutual agreement. The Americans pay an annual rent of $4,085, but although Castro cashed the cheque in the first

Above: exhibit at the quirky Museo Zoológico de Piedra, Boquerón

year of the Revolution, none have been cashed since. Indeed, for all Cubans, the US's presence is a bitter pill to swallow – for them, the base is illegal and an affront to national honor.

From the lookout you can peer across the razor wire and the most intensely mined strip in the world toward notorious Camp Delta, the prison used for alleged Al Qaeda terrorists. There's an international shipping channel through the base. At the height of the Cold War Soviet warships carrying nuclear warheads passed through here.

The Road to Baracaoa

Back at the main turn-off, continue along the road towards Baracoa. This runs through increasingly harsh scenery of desiccated hills and scrubland and then along a dramatic coast with tamarind trees and dark sandy beaches. The road swings inland through Cuba's desert region, and then on as far as **Playa Cajobabo**. Beyond here the highway goes up in tight hairpins through the **Sierra del Purial** mountains, on one of

Cuba's most magnificent routes, **La Farola**. The spectacular views can be obscured by mist, especially in summer, but you'll always see masses of subtropical vegetation and roadside hawkers selling fruit, home-grown coffee, delicious, unsweetened cocoa powder and a regional specialty, *cucuruchos* – cones of sticky shredded coconut mixed with fruit, beautifully packaged in palm leaves. Do not buy the necklaces of colorful snail shells – they're made of *polymita* land snails, an endangered endemic group that is protected by national and international law.

Above: cutting sugar cane on the road to Baracoa. **Right:** roadside fruit sellers

Cross the 450m (1,475ft) Alto de Cotilla pass and drop down to **Baracoa**, an untidy but historic town beautifully sited on a spit of land that curls out into the sea, and backed by the tabletop mountain of **El Yunque** (The Anvil).

To the Top of El Yunque

Go straight to El Castillito within the ruins of an 18th-century fortress that tops the hill in the center of town for a grand view of this setting. But if you think the view of El Yunque from Baracoa is a classic, it's even better the other way round, so set out early the next morning for the **Parque Nacional El Yunque** to hike to the summit. Arrange a guide the night before you go: you could call Francisco Reyes Fonseca from Flori-fauna, who speaks a little English (tel: 0121-42718; $13).

The starting point is **Campismo El Yunque**, 8.5km (6 miles) from the center of Baracoa. Head along the road to Moa for 4km (2½ miles), then turn off left toward the Finca Duaba and branch left after 200m/yds along the rutted dirt track. Aim to be here for 8am. You need to be fit, as the path is steep and can get slippery with mud, so wear good footwear, and come prepared for heat or cold – bring water, sun cream, a warm top and a waterproof coat, as well as insect repellent. The climb will take nearly two hours, along a shady path. At the top you'll find a bust of Antonio Maceo enjoying the view over the cliff-face that plunges toward the plain and Baracoa's bay. Behind him, row upon row of forested ridges stretch to the horizon. Calculate on five hours to make the round trip from Baracoa, including a dip in the limpid waters of the River Duaba, at the end of the hike.

The Soft Option

If you'd like a more relaxing option for the morning, take a car (or a taxi; US$23 round trip) to **Playa Maguana**, a 30-minute drive north along the coast *(see page 70)*. Have lunch at the hotel, returning in the early afternoon.

In the afternoon, stroll around the town, enjoying the laid-back atmosphere and checking out the main sites. *Baracoenses* are proud of their town's rich history, although they have ceded one of their most famous previous claims – that this was the site of Columbus's first landfall in Cuba in 1492 – to Bariay on the northern coast of Holguin Province. Columbus did

Above: Playa Maguana
Right: statue of Columbus

el oriente

land here, later that same year, and a relic linked to him, the **Cruz de Parra**, can be found in the run-down, 19th-century **Iglesia de Nuestra Señora de la Asunción** on the main square. This cross was brought over from Spain by the great navigator and planted on these shores, to be discovered many years later, wrapped in the vine (*parra*) that gave it its name.

Tests by Belgian scientists in the 1980s proved the cross was fashioned not in Spain, but from the native seagrape *(Cocoloba diversifolia)*. However, carbon-dating *did* place it around the era of Columbus, and as such it could well be the earliest Christian relic from the New World. According to 18th-century documents, it once stood 2.65m (8 ft 8in) tall, but is now considerably reduced, and is housed in a glass case, its edges protected by silver strips to prevent the depredations of splinter-stealing pilgrims. Staring defiantly at the church is a bust of Hatuey *(see pages 11 and 70)*, Cuba's first rebel, who some claim was killed here .

Baracoa was Cuba's first town, founded by Diego Velázquez in late 1511 or early 1512, and it was the capital until 1515, when Santiago was founded. It then experienced times of neglect and cycles of economic boom and bust. Before 1966, when completion of La Farola provided a road link with Santiago, Baracoa was known for its isolation, illiteracy, hunger and unemployment.

Explore all this further at the **Museo Municipal** in the **Fuerte Matachín** (fort) on Calle Martí, at the entrance to town (8am–noon, 2–6pm; tours in English; admission fee). Here you'll find an indigenous stone idol, the Idolo de Maguana, along with items from the region's natural history, including a collection of *polymita* snail shells – one of the species is already extinct.

Baracoa has a thriving community of painters, too, and it's worth dropping in to the studio of Roel

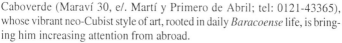

Caboverde (Maraví 30, e/. Martí y Primero de Abril; tel: 0121-43365), whose vibrant neo-Cubist style of art, rooted in daily *Baracoense* life, is bringing him increasing attention from abroad.

Baracoa is one of the only places in Cuba to have a distinctive and tasty regional cuisine. West African in origin, it has coconut oil at its heart, as in its Santa Bárbara sauce, which also uses chilli, garlic, onions and the red colorant, *achiote*. Sea crabs *(jaibas)*, land crabs *(cangrejos)*, conch *(cobo)* or shrimps *(camarones)* cooked in a creamy coconut sauce *(en leche de coco)* all make good options. This cuisine is not easy to track down. The restaurant in El Castillito hotel always has some on the menu – try *calalú*, a rich dish of spinach cooked in coconut oil with pieces of fish or meat. La Punta, in the town's third fortress at the point of the spit, will prepare a wide range of dishes if you ask the day before (7am–9.45pm; tel: 0121-45224). So, too, will the Restaurant-Bar La Colonial, a *paladar* at Martí 123 (10am–11pm; tel: 0121-45391), with its Caribbean-style veranda, friendly service and changing menu.

Above: bust of Hatuey, Baracoa

BEST OF THE BEACHES *(see pull-out map)*

Like most Caribbean islands, Cuba is blessed with some beautiful sandy beaches, particularly on its off-shore cayes. Some have developed tourist infrastructures, and the larger resorts take euros as well as dollars. For recommendations and the key to the $ hotel rates shown here, *see* Accommodation, page 91.

Varadero

This is Cuba's busiest, most developed international resort, comprising a host of hotels and nightclubs along a swathe of beach, stretched along the Hicacos Peninsula, 140km (87 miles) east of Havana (45 mins; approx $25 in a taxi, depending on how far down the peninsula your hotel is). There are good options for kids, and you can hire clubs to play at one of Cuba's few golf courses.

Cayo Largo del Sur

Lying off the south coast, this island is another upscale international resort, offering glorious beaches and a fine selection of watersports, diving, fishing and trips in glass-bottomed boats. It's best booked as a package (including flight) from Havana, and day-trips are possible if you don't have time to stay. You can also fly here from Santiago and the Isla de la Juventud.

Cayo Coco and Cayo Guillermo

These two resort cayes (islands) are linked by a causeway and have fine white-sand beaches, warm, shallow seas, and nature reserves where flamingos feed. They lie to the north of Ciego de Avila province in central Cuba and are linked to the mainland by causeway. Cayo Coco has five resort hotels, and Guillermo four, which, with a new international airport on Cayo Coco, are likely to expand. The best place in Cayo Guillermo is the enchanting Playa Pilar, with beautiful sugary sand, scenic dunes and a great snorkeling site, Cayo Media Luna, just offshore. It's due for development, so get there while it remains unspoilt, if you can.

Above: selling snacks on the beach at Varadero

Playa Santa Lucía

This comprises a string of mid-range, Cuban-run resort hotels strung out along a 20km (12-mile) beach 110km (68 miles) east of Camagüey. It lacks buzz and glamor, but the brilliant-white sands are superb, and not far offshore is one of the country's best reefs, with great diving. At **La Boca**, 8km (5 miles) west, there's a good beach, a couple of restaurants and the chance to take a supervised dive with sharks. Most visitors get bussed in from Holguín airport, nearly 3hrs away, but Camagüey's airport is closer (less than 2 hrs). Cubataxi charges $48 one-way from Camagüey (tel: 0132-298721, 281247).

Guardalavaca and Playa Esmeralda

These beach resorts – two of the very best in Cuba – are about one hour's drive from Holguín airport. Guardalavaca's swathe of white sand is one of the broadest in the country. Next to Guardalavaca is Playa Esmeralda, a beach that's even more alluring.

María La Gorda

Fantastic diving opportunities and a great beach lure people to this far-western region; and a trip here links well with Itinerary 5 *(see page 37)*. There's only one place to stay: the delightful María La Gorda hotel (tel: 0182-778131; fax: 778077; e-mail: recepcion@mlagorda.co.cu; travellers' cheques or cash only; $$$). Modern pine cabins are set on boardwalks in the semi-deciduous woodland. Single dives cost $35, or you can do a five-day course for $365. The hotel is popular (especially Dec–Feb), so book at least a week in advance. It's nearly five hours from Havana ($125 in taxi); or just over two from Pinar del Río ($55); there's also a bus from Havana. From March to April land crabs invade the roads in their thousands and their

claws can spell disaster for your tyres – there is a repair service at the hotel, but make sure your spare is in good condition.

The hotel is on the **Península de Guanahacabibes** (pronounced *wa-na-ca-beeb-ez*), one of Cuba's finest spots for birds and wildlife. It's a Biosphere Reserve, centered on the Parque Nacional Guanahacabibes, with guided trails ($6–$10 per person). Organize these at the information center at La Bajada.

Cayo Levisa

With its first-rate, 3km (2-mile) beach, this beautiful mangrove-covered caye makes a great destination, or links well with Itinerary 5 *(see page 37)*. There's

Right: beach at María La Gorda

an appealing small-scale resort hotel, Hotel Cayo Levisa (book in advance, tel: 0182- 334238, 756501; fax: 756505; $$$), with 40 cabins amid the pines, seagrapes and coconut palms that fringe the beach. Ask for one of the new cabins, which have little balconies and an airy feel. The hotel runs trips to some great dive and snorkeling sites nearby, as well as to deserted Cayo Paraíso, about which Ernest Hemingway wrote in *Islands in the Stream.* You can rent kayaks, catamarans and aqua bikes.

It's a 25-minute trip by boat from Palma Rubia on the mainland to Cayo Levisa: get to the quay by 9.45am at the latest to catch the 10am boat, or there's another departure at 6pm. Boats back leave Cayo Levisa at 9am and 5pm. The boat is free if you are staying at the hotel, otherwise it's $15 for a one day round trip.

Playa Maguana

Palm-fringed Playa Maguana is an idyllic, tranquil beach 20km (12 miles) north of Baracoa *(see page 66)*, about a 30-minute drive along a rough road, past the River Toa. It has only one hotel, the secluded Villa Maguana (tel: 0121-45165; $$), with four rooms (all with air conditioning and satellite TV), although another 12 are planned.

Cayo Sabinal

The beach's slogan, 'All routes lead to Sabinal,' is not entirely honest. There's only one road and a bad one at that, but it's a fine place to get away from it all, though you have to walk out 550m/yds to the deep water. Rustic cabins are available at Playa Los Pinos ($) for a good-value $25 per

person, including breakfast and dinner. This price may change when 20 new cabins are completed. Reservations can be made via Rumbos offices in Santa Lucía or Camagüey (tel: 0132-297229, 294807; e-mail: oscar@ camaguey.rumbos.cu). Drive carefully on the unsurfaced roads.

Jardines de la Reina

This archipelago of almost 700 genuinely virgin *cayes*, lying to the south of the provinces of Ciego de

Avila and Camagüey, is an expensive and exclusive destination for sport fishermen and divers. It's Cuba's largest marine national park, protecting 2,170sq. km (837sq. miles). Most people who visit come for the catch-and-release fly-fishing for species such as bonefish and tarpon.

Visits are organized as week-long packages ($$$$) that must be arranged well in advance. Accommodations are in a floating hotel moored near Cayo Anclitas. The boat to the hotel leaves Júcaro (30 minutes by car south of Ciego de Avila) on Saturday, returning Friday; and the trip out takes about 2½hrs. For more information, contact Avalon (www.avalons.net) or Roxton Bailey Robinson Worldwide (www.rbrww.com).

Isla de la Juventud

With perhaps the best diving in the country, the island is primarily a destination for sub-aqua fans, but it also has some fine beaches and interesting wildlife. There's only one place to stay worth recommending: the all-inclusive Hotel Colony resort, 42km (26 miles) southwest of the capital Nueva Gerona (tel: 046-398181, 398282; fax: 398420; e-mail: reservas@colony.co.cu; $$$), where you'll find the Centro Internacional de Buceo (International Diving Center). Comfortable cabins are well equipped, and there are great sunsets; but bring repelent for the insects.

Recommended are the daily diving excursions ($35/day) to the **Punta Francés Marine Reserve**, 45 minutes by boat from the hotel, to see corals, sponges, reef sharks, turtles, barracudas and moray eels. A five-day ACUC diving course costs $365 excluding accommodations.

You can also explore the rest of the island for a day: visiting the prison where Fidel Castro was incarcerated after the Moncada attack – the Presidio Modelo near Nueva Gerona (Mon–Sat 8am–4pm, Sun 8am–noon; admission fee); and taking a tour to Punta del Este in the south of the island, where there's a pristine beach and indigenous rock art. This latter trip goes into a restricted military zone, and must be arranged in advance via the efficient Ecotur agency in Nueva Gerona (C/. 39 s/n e/. 24 y 26; tel: 0146-327101; ecoturpineroij@yahoo.es).

Cubanacán flies twice daily to Nueva Gerona from Havana ($64 return).

Top Left and Left: the lovely Cayo Levisa
Above: watersports

Leisure
Activities

SHOPPING

Throughout Cuba you'll find a plethora of souvenir stores that sell standard-issue Che Guevara items and overpriced postcards. However, Cuba also produces world-class music, art, cigars and rum, as well as some excellent *artesanía* (handicrafts). These are sold in state-run stores and co-operatives, plus markets and individual artists' studios. Leather goods, linen, traditional *guayabera* shirts, high-quality carvings in Cuban hardwoods, attractive ceramics, musical instruments, jewelry, colored Tiffany-style glass, fans and jolly *papier-mâché* children's toys are just some of the things that are worth looking for.

Export Regulations

Works of art need an export certificate, preferably from the gallery that sold it to you or, if not, the National Registry of Cultural Works (Registro Nacional de Bienes Culturales, Calle 17 No 1009, e/. 10 y 12, Vedado) or branches of the Fondo Cubano de Bienes Culturales. There are also export controls on antiquities and books that are more than 50 years old. Ask for official export receipts and invoices if you're buying art or antiquities from state galleries. An export certificate costs $10 and allows you to take out up to five works – but can sometimes take several days to process.

Where to Shop

In Old Havana, the best place to start your browsing is the Feria de la Catedral on Calle Tacón (Wed–Sat 9am–6pm), but also check out such places as the nearby Palacio de Artesanía, at Cuba 64 esq. Tacón. Both Obispo and Mercaderes streets have interesting shops; and antiquarian and secondhand books can be found in the Plaza de Armas (Wed–Sat 9am–6pm). There are also a number of art galleries in an around the Plaza de la Catedral, and contemporary art at the Casa de los Condes de Jaruco in the Plaza Vieja.

In Central Havana, there's an arts and handicraft gallery in the southern wing of the Capitolio, and the Prado holds a worthwhile arts fair every Sunday. Vedado has a handicrafts market, the Feria del Malecón, at Malecón e/. D y E (Tues–Sun 9am–5pm). José Martí international airport has a good selection of stores and sells a wide variety of books, ranging from literature to studies of Afro-Cuban religion.

If you would like to take home some of the great sounds of Cuba, CDs are a good buy. They are widely available these days, but Artex and Egrem outlets often have the best choice. Most places will happily let you listen before you buy. There's an Egrem store in Central Havana at Galiano (also called Avenue Independencia) e/. Concordia y Neptuno; and one in Santiago, at José Saco (Enramada) 309, e/. San Felipe y San Pedro.

Cigars

You'll be approached a thousand times on the street during your stay and asked whether you want to buy cigars. Vendors will tell you how they have a friend who works in a tobacco factory, or something similar. These stories aren't *always* lies, but usually what you're sold are copies – they look realistic but are made of poor quality tobacco or con-

Left: souvenirs galore, El Morro
Right: miniature mementoes

Rum

Rum is to Cuba what whisky is to Scotland – Cuban rums have one of the finest reputations in the world and a bottle makes an excellent gift. Younger rums tend to be used for mixing in *mojitos* or *cuba libres*, but the smooth, aged rums make great sipping drinks too. Havana Club is the most famous brand internationally and comes in a range of ages, from young rums like the transparent Silver Dry through to the seven-year-old dark *añejo* version costing about $15 a bottle. Real connoisseurs can splash out $85 on a bottle of 15-year-old Havana Club *Gran Reserva*.

There are many other excellent brands worth sampling during your stay on the island – Caney, Santiago de Cuba and Matusalem, for example. Each has its own personality and if you find one you like, buy a bottle – most types are difficult to track down abroad.

Prices

Cuba is certainly not the least expensive Latin American country to visit, and you may be surprised at how much money you can get through. You can economize to some extent by trying to get into the Cuban pesos economy (buying street food, for example), but generally you'll be charged in US dollars for everything you buy.

tain things like banana leaves. In addition to this, these fakes will in all probability be confiscated at the airport on your exit unless you can provide an official receipt. So, the safe option is to buy only in official stores.

The best cigars will bear the legend *Hecho en Cuba. Totalmente a mano* – 'Made completely by hand in Cuba' – stamped on the box and will have an official holographic seal. Machine-made cigars are also available – they're much less expensive, but are not of the same high quality. The best cigars – such as Cohiba *Espléndidos* – cost around US$350 for a box of 25, but $100–$150 will buy you a box of good quality alternatives. Ask in one of the specialist stores if you're not sure what to buy and need advice: there's one with an excellent choice in the specialist cigar hotel, the Conde de Villanueva at Mercaderes 202, esq. Lamparilla, La Habana Vieja. Otherwise try the nearby Casa Museo del Habano, Mercaderes 120 e/. Obispo y Obrapía; or try the store in the Partagás factory, behind the Capitolio.

When leaving Cuba, you should keep your cigars in your hand luggage, along with both copies of the official receipt, one of which will be retained by customs.

Above: Cuba's most famous product
Right: weighing the raw material

EATING OUT

Don't come to Cuba if you're in search of gourmet travel – gastronomy is not the country's forte. It is improving, however, often with the input of foreign-owned hotel chains, and sometimes you can be surprised by a really excellent meal.

If you're staying in a *casa particular*, your best bet is to eat there. Virtually all of them serve meals (they pay a compulsory tax, whether they want to serve meals or not, so it makes sense to do so) and offer some of the best food in Cuba. They can only serve guests staying with them; and remember that it's illegal for them to serve lobster *(langosta)* and shrimps *(camarones)* – nothing will happen to you if an inspector arrives, but the authorities will fine the owner US$1,500 and revoke their licence. Many owners take the risk – if they do, be discreet.

Small private restaurants known as *paladares,* once found everywhere, are now less common. High taxes and heavy fines have finished many off. Although there are some classics, many don't live up to expectations. Hotel buffets are often insipid affairs.

The chances are that you'll be eating a lot of Cuban Creole fare *(comida criolla)*, revolving around pork *(puerco)*, chicken *(pollo)* and the rice-and-beans mix called *moros y cristianos* (Moors and Christians) or *arroz congrí*. A *bifstec* tends to be pork, not beef, which is scarce and expensive. As well as rice, fried plantain is a common and tasty ingredient – you may be offered *chicharritas* (thinly-sliced) or *tostones* (thick chunks, flattened). Other things you will come across are *vianda* (starchy root vegetables), such as *malanga*, yucca and sweet potato *(boniato)*.

There is some excellent seafood, although you'll find that delicate dishes such as lobster can be overcooked or drowned in heavy sauces. One of the best ways to get your lobster is *a la plancha* – grilled on a hot plate.

Short of salads, vegetarian food is difficult to track down. Bottled water is widely available; and you'll find wines in many restaurants – most of it imported from Spain.

If your stomach isn't too delicate, give the street food a try. It's generally a hit-and-miss affair (a hit because you get to meet some great Cubans, though mainly a miss in culinary terms), but try to find a good peso pizza.

If you're in Manzanillo, try the *ceviche de ostiones* – fresh oysters marinated with lime juice, chilli and tomato. Not what your standard travel doctor would advise, but *deeelicious.*

Restaurants

Havana
1830 Restaurante/Bar
Malecón y Calle 20, Vedado
Tel: (07) 55-3090/91/92
A swish restaurant with an ambitious menu, including such rarely-sighted dishes as beef carpaccio. The Creole food is well priced, but some of the lobster main courses go up to a whopping $37. Open noon–11.45pm. There's an open-air club behind the restaurant.

Barrio Chino
Zanja e/. Rayo y San Nicolás, Centro Habana
Not a single restaurant, but one tiny, colorful street crammed with Chinese restaurants. There's plenty of atmosphere, with red lanterns. Half a block away, at Dragones 355–357 e/. Manrique y San Nicolás, is Los Tres Chinitos (open daily till late, 24hrs Thur–Sun; tel: (07) 863-3388). It's popular and serves vast, good-value portions. Ask to be directed as it's a bit of a maze, with separate sections serving different menus.

Right: old-style bar, Camagüey

Bodeguita del Medio

Empedrado 207, La Habana Vieja
Tel: (07) 867-1374

Crowded tourist venue, but with bohemian atmosphere and walls plastered with graffiti of the famous and not-so-famous. Photos of illustrious patrons of yesteryear – the likes of Miguel Matamoros, Nicolás Guillén, Nat King Cole and, of course, Papa Hemingway. Open noon–midnight; bar till 2am.

Cervecería Taberna de La Muralla

San Ignacio esq. Muralla, Plaza Vieja
Tel: (07) 866-4453

A bright, modern, tourist-oriented Cuban version of a beer hall, serving Austrian-style home-brewed beer, bar snacks and meat from the charcoal grill outside. If you're thirsty, order one of their $12 beer 'towers.'

La Divina Pastora

Fortaleza de San Carlos
Tel: (07) 860-8341

High-quality seafood is served at this restaurant at the foot of the fortress, but you will have to shell out – $22 for a *mar y tierra* seafood and meat platter. Open noon–11pm.

Paladar Doña Blanquita

1st floor of El Prado 158 e/. Colón y Refugio
Tel: (07) 867-4958

A twinkly-pink stalwart stuffed with kitsch statuettes and Santería objects, which serves substantial *criollo* fare for about $10 a main course – basically a selection of pork, pork and more pork, with some chicken. Try to get one of the tables on the balcony that overlooks the Prado. Open noon–11pm.

Paladar Doña Carmela

Comunidad No 1, Casa 10
Tel: (07) 863-6048, 867-7472

Near Fortaleza de San Carlos de la Cabaña in Habana del Este, this is an excellent *paladar* with a wide choice of seafood, served in pleasant garden surroundings. Set price of $35.

Paladar La Guarida

Concordia 418 e/. Gervasio y Escobar
Tel: (07) 264-4940

A famous, atmospheric *paladar* that figured in the Cuban hit movie, *Fresa y Chocolate*. Serves tasty *criollo* food. Main courses $12. Open noon–4pm and 7pm–midnight.

Paladar Los Amigos

Avenida M, e/. 19 y 21, Vedado
Tel: (07) 830-0880

Filling *criollo* food, but reserve in advance or arrive early in the evening, as there can be a line for tables. Open till midnight.

Santo Angel

Teniente Rey esq. San Ignacio
Tel: (07) 861-1626

Offers tasteful terrace dining on the Plaza Vieja, with seafood a specialty (a lobster costs $25). There's also a three-course vegetarian menu for $16. Open noon–11pm.

Varadero
Mesón del Quijote

Avenida las Américas
Tel: (0145) 667796

A jolly restaurant with a Spanish theme next door to the El Castillito water tower. Meals

are reasonably priced and options include grilled lobster ($12) and eat-all-you-like paellas ($4–$13). Open noon–midnight.

Restaurante Esquina Cuba
Calle 36 y 1ra Avenida
Tel: (0145) 614019
An open-sided, thatched *bohío* in the center of Varadero town. Its typical Cuban *criollo* cuisine is tasty, and the band plays traditional music. Open 10am–midnight.

Viñales
Casa de Don Tomás
Salvador Cisneros 140
Tel: 018-7936300
Lovely, breezy wooden house, which specializes in a paella-like dish known as Las Delicias de Don Tomás. Open 10am–10pm.

Mural de la Prehistoria
Tel: 018-796260
This thatched tourist restaurant serves mouthwatering roast pork. It's quieter in the evening, when you can dine beneath the floodlit mural. Open 8am–9pm.

Trinidad
El Mesón del Recogidor
Simón Bolívar 424
Tel: 01419-6572/6573
Criollo cuisine in a colonial building with a beautiful patio, near the Plaza Mayor.

Restaurante del Jigüe
Rubén Villena esq. Piro Guinart
Tel: (0419) 4315, 6476
Local *criollo* food in an elegant restaurant on the Plaza del Jigüe. Open 9am–10pm.

Sol y Son
Simón Bolívar 283, e/. Frank País y José Martí
A popular *paladar* in the historic center, serving hearty *criollo* staples. It's often busy with groups, so get there early.

Camagüey
La Campana de Toledo
Plaza San Juan de Dios
Linked to the snack bar at the Parador de los Tres Reyes, with a lovely courtyard garden. Open 10am–9pm.

El Cardenal
Martí 309, e/. Hospital y San Antonio
An excellent-value *paladar*, serving vast portions of chicken and pork, with ample side salads. Food served till 11pm.

Santiago
Don Antonio
Plaza Dolores
Tel: (0122) 652205
There are plenty of places around the Plaza Dolores – just pick the one that best suits your mood. Creole food is served in this wonderful colonial building.

El Cayo
Cayo Granma
Tel: (0122) 641769, 690109
A charming seafood restaurant on stilts, on the small island of Cayo Granma, in the middle of Santiago Bay. It can be reached by ferry from the Embarcadero Ciudamar jetty, 2km (1 mile) from El Morro. Open 11am–9pm.

Santiago 1900
Bartolomé Masó 354 e/. Hartmann y Pío Rosado
Tel: (0122) 623507
A bit erratic in terms of the choice available – it's mainly pork-based *criollo* fare – but the place is splendid, in the former residence of the Bacardí family.

Left: dining al fresco
Above: a *mojito* at the ready

eating out

ENTERTAINMENT & NIGHTLIFE

Cuba positively pulsates with music, rhythm and dance, ranging from trios that play traditional *son, guarachas* and *boleros* in tourist restaurants through to internationally renowned Afro-Cuban folkloric groups, ballet troupes and full-scale cabarets. There are some highly creative theater groups, which are worth seeing if your Spanish is good; but above all, Cuba is famous for its astounding depth of musical talent. It's not just salsa, either – one moment you can be sitting back enjoying an ethereal performance of baroque classical music, the next shaking your stuff to some fierce Afro-Cuban *rumba*. Younger Cubans are much keener on rap and rock than salsa or the back-catalogue of the Buena

Vista Social Club, so you will track down something to fit your tastes.

You're bound to visit one or more *Casa de la Trova* – every city has one, and they all deliver high-quality traditional music. Most are directed at the tourist market, but in some smaller towns they're still faithful to their origins as a place where Cubans get together for spontaneous performances of song and dance. Keep your ears to the ground, too, in case you hear of a *peña* –

a non-touristy party usually involving music, song and sometimes poetry. Cubans have an infectious party spirit, and never seem to need an excuse to celebrate – all they need is a few dollars and a couple of bottles of rum.

You pay an entrance of a few dollars to many places with live music, and this sometimes includes your first drink *(consumo)*. At certain nightclubs you pay an entrance fee but you get a free bar for the night, as long as you stick to Cuban-made drinks.

One thing you can't escape at some point during your stay is *jineterismo*. The term comes from the Spanish word for jockey, and can encompass everything from looking to earn commissions by finding tourists a *casa particular* or selling fake cigars, all the way through to prostitution. *Jineteras* are women who seek to attach themselves to single foreign men either for prostitution or in the hope that they might get an exit visa – they can be quite persistent in places like Santiago and in certain clubs. Single women tourists are likely to get similar treatment from *jineteros* at times.

Havana

In Havana, get a copy of the free listings magazine, the *Guía del Ocio*, available at Infotur offices and some hotels. Find out what's on at the Teatro Nacional on the Plaza de la Revolución, and the Gran Teatro on the Parque Central. If it's classical music you're after, look for concerts by the Camerata Romeu – a chamber orchestra that performs in the Antigua Iglesia de San Francisco de Asís – or Ars Longa, a baroque ensemble based in the Antigua Iglesia de San Francisco de Paula.

Ballet Nacional de Cuba

Gran Teatro, Prado 458, e/. San Rafael y San José
Tel: (07) 835-2948 (Theatre), (07) 861-3077 (Ballet)
Cuba's world-class ballet company performs in the opulent Gran Teatro when not on tour, as do two notable contemporary dance troupes, Danza Contemporánea de Cuba and DanzAbierta. Tickets ($20) can be bought at the Gran Teatro ticket office Mon–Fri 9am–5pm or 1 hour before the show.

Above: a rap artist in Havana

Casa de la Música
Galiano (also called Avenida Independencia) e/. Concordia y Neptuno, Centro Habana.
Tel: (07) 862-4165
A loud and lively indoor venue run by Egrem, the state record company, where modern bands ranging from rock to salsa line up to play to some 400 people. $5 will get you into a matinée performance (4–8pm), but expect to pay up to $25 to see a well-known band in the evening (10pm–4.30pm).

Casa de la Música
Calle 20, 3308, esq. 35, Miramar
Tel: (07) 204-0447
This other Casa de la Música is much farther out from the center. It's popular with Cubans, too, mainly for its live salsa bands. Open midnight–2am or 3am. High entrance fee: $15–20.

Conjunto Folklórico Nacional 'El Palenque'
Patio de la Rumba, Calle 4, e/. Calzada y 5ta, Vedado
Tel: (07) 833-4560, 830-3060
One of the country's best folkloric dance ensembles, whose shows you can catch every Saturday at 3pm.

Café Cantante
Teatro Nacional, Paseo y 39, Plaza de la Revolución
Tel: (07) 873-5713, 874-6011, 879-3558
Popular with Cubans and well worth checking out for its live music and dancing, most afternoons as well as evenings.

La Zorra y El Cuervo
Calle 23, e/. N y O, Vedado
Tel: 07-662402
Long-standing jazz favorite in a basement on La Rampa. Open 10pm–3am.

Los Jardines de 1830
Malecón y Calle 20, Vedado
Tel: (07) 55-3090/91/92
Behind the 1830 Restaurante, this is an open-air venue that's popular among young Cubans with access to dollars (open till 2 or 3am; admission fee). They play a variety of modern international music, and there's live music on Sunday (4–8pm).

Los 12 Apóstoles
El Morro
A modern dance club and bar, favored by tourists and a young, hip Cuban set. It's scenically sited underneath the walls of El Morro – you can down *cuba libres* amongst the vast cannon that face out across the bay.

Tropicana
Calle 72, 4504 e/. 41 y 45, Marianao
Tel: (07) 267-1717
For the grandest cabaret extravaganza in Cuba, head out to Havana's world-famous Tropicana – the original club of an expanding brand. Tickets cost from $65–85, including a quarter-bottle of rum and a mixer. Book at your hotel reception or buy tickets at the entrance between 8.30 and 9pm, the time to arrive if you have paid for the dinner option. The razzamatazz hi-kicks-off at 10pm and the show lasts 1hr 45mins, after which you can head to the club.

Camagüey
Teatro Principal
Padre Valencia 64, e/. Tata Méndez y Lugareño
Tel: 0132-291991 for information
This elegant, historic building hosts important cultural events.

Casa de la Trova
Calle Cisneros y Martí
Parque Ignacio Agramonte has live *son,*

Right: Tropicana show-girl

trova or Afro-Cuban music, depending on the night (Tues–Thur 9pm–midnight, Fri–Sun 9pm–2am; reserve tables in advance).

Camagüey has some impressive **folkloric** dance or **music troupes** – look out for the Grupo Vocal Desandan, with Haitian influence (they practise in the Centro de Patrimonio in Plaza San Juan de Díos); the Afro-Cuban Grupo Artístico Marajuán (tel: 01322-253134); or the Grupo Folklórico de Camagüey.

Santiago
Tropicana
Autopista Nacional Km 1.5
Tel: (0122) 687090, 642579
Traditional music gets the cabaret treatment in a beautiful open-air setting (Wed–Sun only). Tickets are less expensive than in Havana ($20–30 with one drink included); and if you're not eating, get there for 9.30pm in time for the main show at 10pm.

Ask at the Museo del Carnaval or your hotel if there are any performances of one of the city's main Afro-Cuban folkloric ensembles (*conjuntos folklóricos*) or *tumba francesa* groups. Look for La Caridad de Oriente,

Cutumba, Folklórico Oriente or 19 de Setiembre. Otherwise, the Grupo Abureyé is a smaller but still impressive folklore troupe that gives free music-and-dance performances on Sunday evenings in the Casa Cultural San Pedro, next to the Casa Granda hotel on Parque Céspedes; or you can catch them practising there most evenings from 5.30–8pm *(see pages 81–82)*.

There are several nightclubs in the Meliá Santiago hotel *(see page 95)*, including a rooftop bar and a club that has been elaborately mocked-up to look just like colonial Santiago.

Varadero
La Rumba
Avenue Las Américas
Tel: 0145-668210
Aimed at a young crowd. There is a $10 entrance charge, but consumption of Cuban-produced drinks at the bar is then free. Open 10.30pm–3am.

Mambo Club
Autopista Sur
Situated farther down the peninsula, by the Gran Hotel, this club has live music.

Cabaret Continental
Hotel Internacional
Avenue Las Américas
Tel: 0145-667038
Cabaret show Tues–Sat (8pm for dinner, 10pm for the show; $40 with dinner, $25 without).

Above: dancing the *sábado*
Right: jazz in the open-air

CALENDAR OF FESTIVALS & EVENTS

National holidays
January 1 Liberation Day.
May 1 Labour Day.
July 26 Revolution Day, commemorating the attack on the Moncada garrison in 1953 *(see page 14)*.
October 10 Anniversary of the start of the first War of Independence.
December 25 Christmas Day.

Festivals
During some of the following festivals (Santiago's carnival and the Parrandas in Remedios, for example), accommodations will be at a premium and it is essential to make a reservation as far in advance as possible.

January
January 28 José Martí's birthday.
Cubadanza and FolkCuba Festival of Modern Dance, Havana.

February
Havana Cigar Festival.

March
March 8 International Women's Day.
Vintage Car rallies, Havana, Cienfuegos and Matanzas.

Easter
Easter Festival of Street Dance, Havana. Easter *Semana Santa* celebrations in Trinidad.

April
April 1–4 Baracoa. April 1 sees the annual pilgrimage to the obelisk marking the spot where Antonio Maceo landed in 1895. Carnival celebrations are held in Baracoa, with congas along its Malecón.
April 19 The anniversary of the victory at the Bay of Pigs.
International Festival of Percussion, Havana.

May
Cubadisco, Havana. Festival dedicated to showcasing Cuban talent to the world's recording industry moguls.
Hemingway International Marlin Fishing at Marina Hemingway, Tavará (May–June).

June
International Festival of Rum, Havana.

July
July 21–27 Santiago carnival. The biggest procession is held on the 25th with vibrant *comparsa* groups in full parade, *conga* celebrations, fireworks and all-night partying. Offers the best of Santiago's traditional

Above: putting on a show, El Palenque

music. One type of ensemble unique to the city is the *tumba francesa*, practised by two groups, one of which – La Caridad de Oriente – has been recognised by UNESCO as being of special cultural heritage. They preserve the traditional dance and music popular among free Blacks and slaves in 18th-century Haiti: the heavy drums have their origins in Dahomey and the Congo, but the dances are based on courtly French minuets and quadrilles. Not all slaves participated in the 1791 revolt in Haiti – some accompanied their French masters when they fled to Cuba, and it is they who brought this tradition with them.

September
September 8 Procession of the Virgin of Regla, Havana. The city's patron saint is a dark Madonna from the Iglesia de Nuestra Señora de Regla. For Santería believers, she represents the *orisha* Yemayá, goddess of maternity and the sea. The statue holds a white baby Jesus. On the 8th day of every month the statue is given a mini procession around the patio.
September 8 Pilgrimage to the Basílica de Nuestra Señora de la Caridad del Cobre, Santiago, the holiest shrine in Cuba. For Santería believers, the Virgen del Cobre represents Ochún, the goddess of sweet waters, love, fertility and sensuality.

October
Contemporary Music Festival, Havana.
International Ballet Festival, Havana.

November
November 15 Foundation of Havana festivities. This coincides with Havana's carnival, but the latter is nowhere near as vibrant or interactive as the one in Santiago de Cuba.
Wemilere Festival of African Roots – Afro-Cuban festival at Guanabacoa.
Biennial International Theater Festival, Havana.

December
International Festival of New Latin American Cinema, Havana. Early December. This draws movie stars, directors, critics and film buffs from around the world.
Biennial International Jazz Festival, Havana.
December 16–17 Pilgrimage to the shrine of San Lázaro (the *orisha* Babalú Ayé in Santería) at El Rincón, Havana Province.
December 15 and 24 Parrandas in Remedios. The *parrandas* have their origins in a local priest's attempts, in the early 19th century, to goad more people into attending church. He arranged gangs of young people to go around town creating as much of a cacophony as they could on Christmas Eve with the aim of rousing people from their slumbers.

Several towns and villages of Villa Clara province hold *parrandas*, but the most famous one is held in Remedios. The festivities are now essentially a secular affair, an excuse for the two halves of the town, San Salvador and El Carmen, to battle it out over who can design the most spectacular *trabajo de plaza* (tower of light), the most creative floats and throw the best party. Revelers parade with homemade lanterns, and fireworks – hand-made in the local factory – add excitement.

The biggest nights of the festival are December 15 and, above all, the 24th, when the partying goes through the night. If you can't be here on either of these dates, try catching one of the *repiques* (percussion groups) that practise on Sunday nights for two or three months before the festival.

Above: film is a popular medium and Latin-American cinema is celebrated in December
Right: poster for Parrandas festival

PARRANDAS REMEDIANAS

Practical Information

GETTING THERE

Air

Scheduled and charter flights fly to Havana, and charter flights operate to several other airports, such as Holguín and Cayo Coco which serve major beach resorts. It's worth checking on the internet for flight-and-accommodations deals in the resorts, as they can be as economical as flight-only prices.

Cubana flies from Gatwick to Havana and Holguín (www.cubana.cu/ingles). Direct flights from the UK take 9–10 hours. The company also operates flights from several other European capitals; Toronto and Montréal in Canada; and Central and South American cities.

Charters from UK: Airtours fly from Manchester to Varadero, Monarch from Gatwick to Holguín and Varadero. Thomas Cook fly from Manchester and Gatwick to Varadero, Cayo Coco and Holguín.

From the rest of Europe, Iberia flies from Madrid (www.iberia.com) and Air France from Paris (www.airfrance.com).

From Canada Air Canada has direct flights to Havana from Toronto (www.aircanada.ca).

There are also scheduled flights from other countries in Latin America and the Caribbean, including Mexico City and Jamaica.

From the US Tour organizers to Cuba for US citizens include Marazul Charters (www.marazulcharters.com, tel: 800-223-5334) and Canada-based USA Cuba Travel (www.usacubatravel.com, tel: 506-459-3355; fax: 506- 459-3844), which specializes in taking US citizens to Cuba.

Other Destinations You can book onward flights to Cayo Largo del Sur with Aerogaviota (tel: 07-203-0686); and to Cayo Santa María via Gaviota Tours (tel: 07-204-4112, 204-4781).

Departure When leaving Cuba, you must be at the airport 3hrs before your departure time. There is a departure tax of US$25.

Left: a classic way to travel
Right: the slow lane in Camagüey

TRAVEL ESSENTIALS

Bring stocks of film with you. Slide film is virtually impossible to track down. Though dollar pharmacies are reasonably widespread in the touristy areas, it makes sense to bring any prescription medicines you need from home, along with supplies of sun cream, tampons and aspirins.

Passport and Visas

All tourists need a tourist card visa, which can be obtained by your travel agent or through the nearest Cuban consulate, either by post, which can be slow, or in person. You will need to show your passport (valid for at least 6 months from date of arrival in Cuba), return air ticket, evidence of accommodations (as a minimum, your first night's reservation in a hotel) and a check or cash to cover the fee (approx $25). Tourist visas are valid for 30 days from arrival and can be renewed for another 30.

US citizens can visit if they prove they have valid humanitarian, cultural, research or educational reasons, by applying for a special license, best done through a specialist tour operator. Daily spending limits apply. For info, visit www.treas.gov/offices/eotffc/ofac/ and the latest State

Department Consular Information sheet on Cuba. Americans can enter Cuba via a third country – Canada, Mexico, Bahamas or Jamaica are logical options – but this is still considered illegal by US authorities. This way they won't need to apply for a visa in advance, but must fill out a tourist card in the airport when making their connecting flight.

Health

Cuban doctors and dentists have a good reputation, and foreigners are treated in dollar clinics where the supply of medicines is much more predictable than in the hospitals where Cubans are treated. Take out adequate health insurance, though, as anything other than initial treatment in emergencies is not free for

foreigners. You don't need any specific inoculations, although it makes sense to be up to date with hepatitis A, tetanus and typhoid shots. Malaria has been eradicated; but there are sporadic outbreaks of dengue fever.

When to Visit

Cuba has a tropical climate and over 330 days of sunshine a year. The best time to visit is winter – November to end April (dry season) – when the average temperature hovers around the low 70°sF (22°C). Summer – May to the end of October – is wet and humid; June to end November is hurricane season. Average temperatures for this period are in low 80°s F (25°C), but it is often well above 86°F (30°C).

Clothing

Lightweight clothing is all you will need for much of the year. Cubans regularly complain of it being cold during their 'winter,' the equivalent to a Northern European summer. However, it's worth having at least one warm top for the evenings; and if you're planning to go hiking in areas such as the Sierra Maestra, you'll need to come properly prepared, as temperatures can fall to the low 40°F (10°C) when it's wet and windy. Long sleeves and trousers are recommended in the areas affected by mosquitoes.

Customs

You are allowed to bring in two bottles of spirits, a carton of cigarettes and up to 50 cigars. Drugs, pornography and subversive materials are all prohibited.

You can take out up to 23 individually-packaged cigars, without producing any official receipt – any more than that and you'll have to produce your official receipts, plus they'll check that the box has the official holographic seal *(see pages 73–4)*. US citizens can only import Cuban cigars (maximum $100) if they've traveled to Cuba with an official license.

An export certificate is required to export works of art; and you cannot take out books that are more than 50 years old, or items considered part of Cuba's historical patrimony.

GETTING ACQUAINTED

Electricity

Most of Cuba runs on a US-style 110V system. There is also 220V, especially in some international hotels. Electric appliances work with flat two-pin plugs. British visitors should bring adaptors from home.

Time

Cuba is on the same time as US Eastern Standard Time, five hours ahead of GMT. Daylight saving applies from the end of March to October.

Geography

Cuba is an archipelago consisting of the mainland, the Isla de la Juventud, and some 4,000 smaller islands and cayes covering

Above: Cubans are a warm and friendly people

110,922 sq. km (42,827 sq. miles), making it bigger than Portugal, but smaller than England. The mainland is the biggest island in the Antilles, stretching some 1,200km (745 miles) from Cabo San Antonio in the west to Punta Maisí in the east. Central Cuba consists of hot lowland plains, but the island has impressive mountains. The grandest – the Sierra Maestra and the Cordillera Nipe-Sagua-Baracoa – are in the east. The Sierra del Escambray is in the area of Cienfuegos and Trinidad; and the Cordillera de Guaniguanico stretches down the northwest flank of Cuba.

Cuba's population is a little over 11 million. The biggest city, Havana, has more than two million inhabitants.

Government & Economy

Cuba is a Communist state. Its Constitution is modeled on the 1936 Soviet Constitution and states that 'all power belongs to the working people.' Though the government claims democratic legitimacy – it scores ratings above 90 percent in the elections – Cuba is, in essence, a one-party totalitarian state.

Fidel Castro is the head of state, President of the Council of State, Prime Minister of the Council of Ministers, head of the Communist Party and also the Commander-in-Chief of the army – although his brother Raúl is in charge of the military on a day-to-day basis. The army is one of the largest in Latin America and plays an important political role.

The country is divided into 14 provinces and one 'special municipality', the Isla de la Juventud.

Cuba's economy is heavily dependent on tourism for its foreign currency earnings, and on its relationship with Venezuela for access to oil. Sugar production has been hard hit by poor investment and price drops on the world market, and many sugar mills have closed in recent years.

Etiquette

Cubans are immensely warm, gregarious and tactile people. Men shake hands on greeting, and it's customary to kiss a woman once on the cheek. If you're speaking in Spanish, address adults with the formal *Usted* form; the informal *tú* form is only used for children and when you're very friendly with someone.

Above: a hummingbird hovers
Right: Castro mural, Baracoa

Cubans move at an unhurried pace, and putting pressure on them tends to be rather counterproductive. Hissing is a way of getting someone's attention. It is not considered rude.

A question '¿Quién es el último?' – is commonly used to find out who is last in the often free-form lines. Sometimes you won't need to join the main line (for example when paying in dollars in airline offices). Ask a security guard if in doubt.

MONEY MATTERS

The official currency is the Cuban *peso convertible* (abbreviated to CUC), which is divided into 100 *centavos*. Converting US dollars into *pesos* incurs a 10 percent charge (correct at time of printing), while UK pounds, Canadian dollars, Euros, and Swiss francs may be exchanged at the market rate, without surcharge, making these the most economical option. Note that travelers' checks and credit cards (including American Express) issued by North American banks will not be accepted. If you hear the term *divisa*, this has traditionally been used to refer the dollar, but literally means 'hard currency'.

Banks give advances on credit cards, and change travelers' checks at commissions of 3–4 percent. Cadeca ($adeca) offices change travelers' checks (on presentation of your passport and the official purchase receipt for your checks) and give advances on credit cards.

American Express travelers' checks and credit cards are not accepted, nor any others issued by US banks. Euros can be used in the major beach resorts.

Tipping
In restaurants, it's customary to tip 10 percent. Some *paladares* in Havana try to include a service charge, but do not feel obliged to pay this – tipping in these places is entirely discretionary. A dollar represents a sizeable tip for carrying your luggage, or to someone who's shown you around a museum. You might like to give more if you've had a good day tour. You don't have to tip in taxis, but rounding up is appreciated.

GETTING AROUND

Air
Havana José Martí International Airport is 20km (12 miles) from Old Havana (24-hr information line, tel: 07-335666 for international flights; 07-335777, 335778, 335779 for domestic). Taxis into the center of Havana cost between $12 and 20.
Santiago Antonio Maceo International Airport is 15 minutes from the city center.
Other useful airports are found at Santa Clara, Camagüey, Holguín, Baracoa, Cayo Largo del Sur, and Nueva Gerona on the Isla de la Juventud.
Cubana de Aviación is the national carrier. Their headquarters are at Calzada de Infanta 53, Vedado (tel: 07-33-4446, 33-4949, 55-1024; Santiago office tel: 0122-651577, 651578, fax: 686258). Book domestic flights early, as the demand is high. Make sure you reconfirm your flight and arrive a full 2hrs before departure or you may lose your flight.
Aerocaribbean have flights to Santiago, Cayo Coco, Cienfuegos and Holguín. Their head office is at Calle 23, 64 esq. P, Vedado (tel: 07-879-7524, 870-4965, 33-5936, 33-4543); there's another branch in Santiago (tel: 0122-687255).
Aerogaviota flies to Cayo Largo del Sur and Cayo Santa María (tel: 07-204-4112).

Train
The train network in Cuba is slow and unreliable, but can be useful on some longer journeys. All tickets must be bought in dollars.

In Havana, you buy your tickets (cash only; bring your passport) from either the office in the main station or from window 1, Estación La Coubre, Avenida del Puerto

Left: the Tren Turístico on the way to the Valle de los Ingenios, near Trinidad

y Ejido (tel: 07-860-3163/4/5), but the trains leave from the main Estación Central de Ferrocarril. It's best to buy them the day before you travel; and be at the station an hour before your train leaves so that your ticket isn't reallocated. There are twice-daily overnight departures for Santiago (12–14hrs officially, but the journey can take longer): the *regular* service costs $30; the more comfortable *especial* service ($62) has air-conditioning. Trains for most other major destinations leave on alternate days (Pinar del Río, Cienfuegos, Sancti Spíritus, Morón, Holguín, Bayamo, Guantánamo); it's often quicker to take the bus.

Bus

There are two main companies in Cuba – Astro and Viazul. Viazul runs a fleet of more modern, reliable and comfortable tourist buses – they're air-conditioned and have onboard restrooms and videos. Its terminal is at Avenue 26 y Zoológico, Nuevo Vedado, tel: 07-881-1413, 881-5652; www.viazul.cu. You have to be there, tickets in hand, at least 30 minutes before departure.

Astro is the less expensive service that most Cubans use – tourists can also buy tickets on Astro buses, but have to pay in dollars. Its buses are especially full during Cuban holidays – July, August and December. Astro buses leave from the Terminal de Ómnibus Nacional ('Terminal Astro'), not far from the Plaza de la Revolución at Avenida de Boyeros 101, e/. Bruzón y 19 de Mayo, Vedado. Check times in advance (tel: 07- 870-3397 for information) and buy tickets a minimum of one hour in advance. In the terminal building you'll find the Agencia de Divisa, the 24-hr agency where tourists buy tickets in foreign currency.

Car

Renting a car is one of the best ways of seeing Cuba. There are agencies of one or more rental companies in every big hotel but it's best to reserve in advance. You need to be over 21, and show your passport and international driver's license. Most deals include unlimited mileage, but check this first. Compulsory insurance *(seguro)* costs $10–15 a day. Check that it's included in the price quoted and ask what the penalty *(franquicia)* is in case of accident.

Prices vary considerably, and there are no low-cost deals on the Internet. **Vía Rentacar** (tel: 07-204-3606, fax: 204-4455) rents out fun Suzuki two-door *jeepicitos*, a high-clearance four-wheel-drive, good on unsurfaced roads and heavy on fuel. Also at the less expensive end are **MiCar** (tel: 07-55-3535, 204-2444); **Transtur** (tel: 07-33-8915, 862-4518); and **Havanautos** (tel: 07-835-3141 /3142).

Gas/petrol *(gasolina especial)* costs $0.90 a liter. Have cash available in case the credit card machines are down.

Roads Signposting is poor, so a good road map is essential. Try to find *Guía de Carreteras* by the Directorio Turístico de Cuba – El Navegante sells copies, at Mercaderes 115 e/. Obispo y Obrapía, Old Havana. Hitchhikers will help you find your way; picking them up is customary and generally safe.

Road rules Always use seat belts. A *pare* (stop) sign means you must come to a complete halt before continuing. Speed limits are strictly enforced by the police – these are 40kph (25mph) in urban areas; 60kph (37mph) in rural areas; 90kph (56mph) on highways and 100kph (62mph) on the expressway. Slow to 40kph (25mph) when passing police control points. Always make sure your spare tyre is in good condition. If

Above: a rental car is one of the best ways to see Cuba

you get a flat, ask for the nearest *ponchera*, and agree a price beforehand – aim for US$1–3 dollars per tyre.

Theft from vehicles can sometimes be a problem in towns. At night, look for an official *parqueo* ($1–3), or ask at your *casa particular* if they know someone who will guard your car for you.

Taxi

There are a bewildering variety of taxis, especially in the cities. Some are not permitted to pick up foreigners. Tourist taxis

can be hailed on the street, but it's often quicker to go to a tourist site or hotel rather than wait for one to pass. Renting a taxi for a day is often an economical alternative to renting a car, but always establish a price before you set off.

Panataxis (tel: 07-555555) and **Habanataxi** (tel: 07-539086) are two of the least expensive Havana companies, charging $0.45/km.
Vintage American vehicles can be hired through Gran Car (tel: 07-41-7980, 57-7338).
Horse-drawn carriages cost $5–$10 per person for an hour's tour of Old Havana.
Cocotaxis (bright yellow two-stroke buggies) buzz around for $0.50/km.
Bicitaxis (bicycle taxis) are not supposed to take foreigners, but many will risk a sizeable fine to get the tourist trade – expect to pay about $1 for a ride within Havana's historical center.

BUSINESS HOURS

Office hours are from about 8.30am–5 or 6pm Mon–Fri, sometimes with an hour's break for lunch. Banks are open Mon–Fri, generally from 8.30am–3pm.

It is not unusual for offices to close early because of blackouts and transportation problems. Dollar retail stores and supermarkets usually open Mon–Sat 9am–5 or 6pm. Neighborhood markets catering to locals open from 8am–noon and 5–7pm.

Top: bicycle taxis awaiting customers
Above: taking things nice and slowly

ACCOMMODATION

Most of the best hotels are owned and operated in part by foreign companies, while those owned wholly by Cuban companies are a mixed bag – some are great, others look in need of some investment and expertise. Often, a hotel's star rating is on the generous side, so don't expect it to be comparable to the same star rating in more developed countries.

Accommodation comes at a wide range of prices. You can usually pick up a double room in a *casa particular (see below)*, for example, for around $15–30, while a double in a luxurious, all-inclusive resort hotel could cost around $190 per person. Check what 'all-inclusive' actually means – you usually pay supplements for using amenities such as the internet, laundry, motorized watersports, diving; but also sometimes the safe box in your room, lobster meals, non-house wines, imported spirits, a sea view and snorkeling.

For more contact with Cubans, stay in *casas particulares* – private homes. Although not all choose to display the sign, most official *casas particulares* identify themselves by means of a blue-and-white sticker with '*Arrendador Inscripto*' written between two vertical chevrons. There is some latitude for bargaining on prices, especially during the low season, but don't expect prices to drop far – the owners have hefty overheads, paying high taxes on each room, whether or not it is actually occupied. Single occupancy is usually charged at the same rate as double; and prices do not usually include breakfast.

It is important to have your passport with you at all times when traveling around Cuba – a photocopy is not sufficient to register at *casas particulares*. Diplomats and accredited businessmen are not allowed to stay in *casas particulares*.

For accommodations in the main resorts, see Itinerary 13, Best of the Beaches *(see pages 68–71)*.

The price key used here is based on a standard double room in high season:

$ = budget ($15–35)
$$ = inexpensive ($36–65)
$$$ = moderate ($66–125)
$$$$ = expensive ($126–200)
$$$$$ = luxury ($201+)

Havana
Hotel Nacional
Calle 21 y O, Vedado
Tel: (07) 855-0294, 873-3564
Fax: (07) 873-5171
E-mail: reserva@gcnacio.gca.cma.net or ejecut@gcnacio.gca.cma.net
An old-style hotel of international class and with plenty of character. It has two pools and a gym, and is sited on a low promontory overlooking Havana's bay and the Monument to the Victims of the Maine. $$$$

Hotel Raquel
Amargura 103 esq. San Ignacio
La Habana Vieja
Tel: (07) 860-8280, Fax: (07) 860-8275
E-mail: habaguanex@hotelraquel.co.cu
Built in 1908 with a stunning art nouveau lobby and only 25 rooms, all with bathtubs. The 24-hour bar is open to non-guests. $$$$

Hotel Santa Isabel
Calle Baratillo 9 e/. Obispo y Narciso López,
La Habana Vieja
Tel: (07) 860-8201, Fax: (07) 860-8391
Exquisite, intimate five-star hotel in the former mansion of the Counts of Santovenia, on the Plaza de Armas. Service is professional; and suites have internet access. There's no pool, but it has the finest hotel patio in Havana, and a huge roof terrace. Reserve, ideally a month in advance. $$$$

Right: Hotel Santa Isabel, Havana

Hostal del Tejadillo
Calle Tejadillo 12 esq. San Ignacio
Habana Vieja
Tel: (07) 863-7283
E-mail:
comercial@habaguanexhtejadillo.co.cu
Located in the historic center, a block from the Plaza de la Catedral. It has a modern, fresh feel. Half the rooms have a small kitchenette with microwave. **$$$**

Hotel Inglaterra
Paseo del Prado 416, esq. San Rafael
Tel: (07) 860-8595/96/97, Fax: (07) 860-8254
E-mail: reserva@gcingla.gca.cma.net
An atmospheric tourist favorite, with an ornate 19th-century lobby and great views from the roof terrace. The rooms fronting the plaza are airier than those farther back, but can be noisy. **$$$**

Convento de Santa Clara
Cuba 610 e/. Luz y Sol
Habana Vieja
Tel: (07) 861-3335, Fax: (07) 665696
E-mail: reaca@cencrem.cult.cu
Nine rooms in a 17th-century convent, plus some multi-bed dormitories. Breakfast included. Worth spending the extra $10 per person for the enormous suite with terra cotta-tiled floor, own terraced balcony and kitchen area (but no crockery). **$$**

Casa de Rafaela y Pepe
San Ignacio 454 e/. Sol y Santa Clara
Tel/Fax: (07) 862-9877, 867-5551
An fine *casa particular* in Old Havana – a high-ceilinged, second-floor apartment full of antiques, one block from the Plaza Vieja. Balconies sprout from all sides; the beds have well-sprung mattresses, the bathrooms are large and clean; and there is a refrigerator. Reserve as far in advance as possible. **$**

Casa de Eugenio Barral
San Ignacio 656 e/. Jesús María y Merced
Tel/Fax: (07) 862-9877
A quiet, airy upper-floor apartment in a colonial house, with a welcoming feel. Antiques lend the place character; the rooms are kept spruce, and there is a shared bathroom. The breakfasts are huge and tasty; but they don't serve evening meals. Reserve early. **$**

Casa de Esther
Aguila 367 e/. Neptuno y San Miguel
Tel: (07)862-0401
E-mail: esthercardoso@hotmail.com
An oasis in the heart of run-down but lively Centro Habana – a well-maintained house with a handy roof terrace. Rooms are airy and comfortable and there is a shared bathroom. Make reservations well in advance. **$**

Varadero
Paradisus Varadero
Off the Autopista Sur
Tel: (0145) 668700, Fax: (0145) 668705/07
www.solmeliacuba.com
The most luxurious of Varadero's all-inclusive resorts. Bungalow-style lodgings, quiet and spacious layout. 421 rooms. Scuba diving included in the price. **$$$$$**

Mansión Xanadú
Carretera Las Américas, Km 8.5
Tel: (0145) 668482, 667750, 667388
Fax: (0145) 668481
E-mail: varaderogolfclub@ip.etecsa.cu
The chic mansion, built in 1930 for Irenée Du Pont, the industrialist, retains many original fittings. Golf green fees are included and guest can use the pool at Meliá Las Américas next door. A restaurant serves international cuisine. There are only six rooms, so reserve at least a month in advance. **$$$$**

Above: Hotel Inglaterra, Havana

Varadero Internacional
Carretera Las Américas
Tel: (0145) 667038, 667039
Fax: (0145) 667246, 667045
E-mail: reserva@gcinter.gca.tur.cu
A less expensive option, in a comfortable, remodeled 1950s hotel that offers a bed-and-breakfast price as well as an all-inclusive one. Smack-bang on a broad stretch of beach. There's also a cabaret. **$$$**

Zapata Peninsula
Bohío Don Pedro
Tel: (0145) 92825, 93224
E-mail: sistema@cienaga.var.cyt.cu
A clutch of good-value, thatched cabins behind the Finca Campesina tourist complex. It's signposted, some 650 m/yds south of the main Havana-Santa Clara highway, on the road to Playa Larga. Cabins have their own bathroom, TV, fan and refrigerator, and there's a small restaurant that, with prior notice, will serve a 6am breakfast to fishermen and early-birders. Mosquitos can be a problem in summer, so bring repelent. **$**

Hotel Guamá
7km (4 miles) by boat from La Boca
Tel: (0145) 92535
E-mail: sistema@cienaga.var.cyt.cu
Characterful thatched indigenous-style *caneyes* and cabins built on stilts on a series of islands that have been interconnected with wooden bridges and have a fine swimming pool. At certain times of year mosquitos will eat you alive, so bring repelent.

Viñales
Los Jazmines
Carretera de Viñales, Km 25
Tel: (018) 796205 or (07) 334238
Fax: (018) 796215
One of three medium-sized hotels in the valley, each with its own distinct character. This one has one of the finest views in Cuba, although you'll have tourist buses pulling up outside because of this. Food is unexciting; but the pool is excellent. The rooms overlooking the pool can be noisy due to the night time entertainment (till 11.30pm) – better to go for one of the little cabins downhill from the pool or a room in the new block, all of which have views. **$$$**

El Rancho Vicente
Carretera Puerto Esperanza, km33
Tel: (018) 796201/21 or (07) 334238
Fax: (018) 796265
E-mail: rrpp@sanv.co.cu
Located 8km/5 miles from Viñales, by the Cueva del Indio. Surrounded by lush vegetation rich in birdlife. Well-fitted-out, private cabins dotted over the hillside. Has a modest pool and a mud-therapy center. **$$**

Casa Eliza
Rafael Trejo 37
Tel: (018) 796028
You'll never be short of a room in Viñales if you just turn up looking for a *casa particular*: there are many so-so options, but no really great ones. Casa Eliza has a small apartment with air-conditioning and TV, as well as its own little terrace; or try **Casa de Ramón y Dulce María**, Salvador Cisneros 81 (tel: 793262). **$**

Las Terrazas
Hotel Moka
Complejo Turístico Las Terrazas
Tel: (0182) 778600 and 778605, or in Havana (07) 204-3739
E-mail: reservas@commoka.get.tur.cu
On a hill overlooking the lake, this white-washed, crescent-shaped hotel is a splendid example of eco-friendly design, blending harmoniously with the surrounding forests. Trees grow through the structure and there's plenty of light and air. All but two rooms have a view of the lake, and some even have views from the bathtub. There's a pool; and the restaurant serves great food. **$$$**

Trinidad
Casa Muñoz
Jesús María / José Martí 401 esq. Olvido / Santiago Escobar
Tel/Fax: (01419) 3673
E-mail: trinidadjulio@yahoo.com
Trinidad is the place to stay in *casas particulares* and this is one of the best in Cuba. The colonial, family-friendly house oozes character, with its *mampara* swing doors, antiques and courtyard. It is owned by a hospitable, English-speaking couple. Julio, an accomplished photographer, arranges photo workshops. Reserve early. **$**

Casa Font
Gustavo Izquierdo 105, e/. Simón Bolívar y Piro Guinart
Tel: (01419) 3683
This is one of Trinidad's most stylish *casas particulares*. Rubén de León Aragón's colonial home could easily be a museum, with its Baccarat crystal chandeliers, *mamparas* and Trinitarian *mediopunto* arches. Enjoyable meals. Reserve as far in advance as possible. $

Casa de Carlos Zerquera
Fernándo Hernández 54
Tel: (01419) 3634
Two excellent rooms in the home of the town's official historian, next to the Museo Romántico. It is a beautiful colonial building dating from the beginning of the 19th century, with three wonderful *vitrales*, a large patio and a facade painted in eye-catching Trinidad green. English and French spoken. Again, reserve early, especially in high season. $

Hostal Julia Ramírez
Simon Bolívar 554 e/.
Rita María Montelier y Juan Márquez
Tel: (01419) 3485
E-mail: ch190302@hotmail.com
Rents one room only, with a private bathroom, in a glorious colonial house with 19th-century antique furniture and a mango tree on the patio. Early reservation is recommended. $

Santa Clara
Hotel Santa Clara Libre
Parque Vidal 6
Tel: (0142) 207548, 217338
No beauty on the outside, but it's wonderfully central, fronting the main square. The rooms that face this way are small and bright; but they can be noisy on weekend nights, as the square buzzes with activity. $$.

Hotel Los Caneyes
Circunvalación y Eucalypto
Tel/Fax: (0142) 218140
Out-of-town option, about 2km (1¼ miles) from the Che Guevara monument and 4km (2½ miles) from Parque Vidal. The rooms are in fun, circular *caneys* – indigenous-style thatched huts – and there is a pool. Can get busy with day-tripping Cuban families on weekends. $$

Hospedaje Laura Torres
Calle Bonifacio Martínez 4
Tel: (0142) 203481
E-mail: lauratg@correo.unam.mx
The best street for *casas particulares*, four-and-a-half blocks south of Parque Vidal, between Serafín García and Morales. Try, too, Casa de Rosalía Reyes at No 8 (tel: 0142-202466). $

Remedios
Hotel Mascotte
Máximo Gómez 117
Tel: (0142) 395144, Fax: (0142) 395723
E-mail: mascotte@civc.inf.cu
Ten rooms, five of which face the main square. All are comfortable, with air-conditioning, satellite TV and minibar and some are enormous (ask for Room 1). Reserve well in advance if coming for the Parrandas. $$

Cayo Coco
Tryp Cayo Coco
Tel: (0133) 301300, Fax: (0133) 301386
www.solmeliacuba.com
A 508-room, upscale all-inclusive resort that's popular with Canadians. Service is stylish and the atmosphere is lively. There's a supplement for upgrading to superior status, which offers more luxurious dining and a later check-out time. There's also a supplement for ocean-view rooms. $$$$$

Above: Casa Granada Hotel, Santiago

Cayo Guillermo
Villa Cojímar
Tel: (0133) 301712, Fax: (033) 301727
E-mail: alojamiento@cojimar.gca.tur.cu
This is a quiet, relatively small, all-inclusive resort hotel with Spanish villa-style reception and 212 rooms. Narrow strip of beach. $$$$

Camagüey
Gran Hotel
Maceo 67, e/. Agramonte y Gómez
Tel: (0132) 292094, Fax: (0132) 293933
Email: reservas@hgh.camaguey.cu
A 1920s hotel that overlooks the main shopping street. The stylish fifth-floor dining salon is light and airy, with chandeliers and good views; but the best views of the city's terra cotta rooftops and churches are from the roof terrace bar. $$

Milagros Sánchez
Cisneros 124, esq Raúl Lamar
Tel: (0132) 297436
Central *casa* with tiled courtyard and flamboyant, kitsch decor; garage. $

Santa Lucia
Gran Club Santa Lucía
Tel: (0132) 336265/3336265
Fax: (0132) 365327/365153
An all-inclusive hotel that makes a good family option, offering eight family suites among its 25 or so rooms. It has a mixed clientele of Europeans and Canadians. The use of catamarans for reaching the reef is free if you know how to sail, otherwise it's $5 with a guide. $$$

Guardalavaca
Brisas Guardalavaca
Calle 2, 1
Tel: (0124) 30218
Fax: (0124) 30418/30162
E-mail: reservas@brisas.gvc.cyt.cu
Comprises two sections, Brisas Las Villas and the Brisas Hotel, both popular with families. The villas are peaceful and relaxing with spacious rooms. The hotel is livelier, with a piano bar and a disco. All the rooms have balconies and the food is a step up from what you'll find in the hotels in Santa Lucia. $$$$

Playa Esmeralda
Paradisus Río de Oro
Tel: (0124) 30090, Fax: (0124) 30095
www.solmeliacuba.com
One of Cuba's most luxurious resorts – all-inclusive and ideal for honeymooners or anyone seeking something a little special. There are three tiny beaches in coves on one side of the complex and the gorgeous swathe of Playa Esmeraldas on the other. The food is high quality. $$$$$

Santiago
Casa Granda
Heredia 201, esq San Pedro
Tel: (0122) 686600, 653021
Fax: (0122) 686035
E-mail: recep@casagran.gca.tur.cu
Listed as a four-star, this grand-looking 1914 hotel has a five-star downtown site, right on the Parque Céspedes, but three-star service. Dimly lit, the rooms are spacious and sound-proofed. The ground-floor café is excellent for people-watching, but head up to the roof terrace bar for a great overview of the square. $$$

Meliá Santiago de Cuba
Avenue de las Américas y Calle M
Tel: (0122) 687070, Fax: (0122) 687170
E-mail: reservas1.msc@solmeliacuba.com
An international quality five-star hotel in a modernist glass-and-steel structure, with friendly service. The rooms are comfortable and classically stylish; though some shower hoses are too short. There are fantastic panoramic views from the 15th-floor bar. The gourmet restaurant offers better value for money than the buffet. $$$$

Hotel Villa Gran Piedra
Carretera a Gran Piedra, Km 14.5
Tel: (0122) 686147/686395
E-mail: recepcion@gpiedra.scu.cyt.cu
A great place to stay if you want to be outside the city, perched up on top of the wooded Gran Piedra ridge. The 22 brick-built cabins sleep 2–4 people. All have satellite TV and balconies, and some have outstanding views out to sea (ask for cabin No 1, or one numbered 14–20). Eco-hiking trails fan out from the hotel for which you can contract guides. $$

Adela Díaz
Heredia 374, esq. Reloj
Tel: (0122) 652696
Central *casa particular* offering a large room
with refrigerator, fan, air-conditioning and
separate private bathroom; plus there's park-
ing nearby on the Plaza de Dolores. $

Raimundo Ocaña
*Heredia 308, e/. Pío Rosado y Porfirio
Valiente*
Tel: (0122) 624097
E-mail: co8kz@yahoo.es
Room with small private bathroom and air-
conditioning, plus a pleasant patio. $

Mireya Gómez
José A Saco 563 e/. Barnada y San Austín
Tel: (0122) 628612
Rather dark room with air-conditioning and
a shared bathroom in a friendly house close
to Plaza de Marte. Use of refrigerator. $

Bayamo
Hotel Royalton
Maceo 53 e/. García y Joaquín Palma
Tel: (0123) 422224, 422290, 422268
Fax: (0123) 424792
E-mail: hroyalton@islazul.grm.tur.cu
Well-sited on the Parque Central. The best
and brightest rooms are the four facing the
main square, all with balconies. $$

Baracoa
Hotel El Castillo
Calixto García s/n, Loma el Paraíso
Tel: (0121) 45165
Fax: (0121) 45223
E-mail: castillo@enet.cu
An attractive three-star hotel with pool, sited
in the ramparts of the town's 18th-century
fortress, with views of the town and El
Yunque. The restaurant has regional dishes
on the menu. $$

Casa Colonial El Mirador
Maceo 86 e/. 24 de Febrero y 10 de Octubre
Tel: (0121) 42647
E-mail: joan@toa.gtm.sld.cu
One of a number of *casas particulares* in
town. A hospitable, airy house close to the
main square, with a balcony overlooking the
town. The host speaks good English. $

HEALTH AND
EMERGENCIES

Hospital
Clínica Central Cira García,
Calle 20, 4101 esq. 41, Playa, Havana
Tel: (07) 204-2811, 2812. 24hrs

Pharmacies
Farmacia Internacional Habana Libre,
L e/. 25 y 23 (8am–8pm)
Farmacia Internacional
Terminal 3, Aeropuerto José Martí, Rancho
Boyeros
Tel: (07) 264105. 24hrs

Emergency Telephone Numbers
Police: 106
Ambulance: (07) 879-5400 (Havana)
Fire: 105
Breakdown: Make sure your car rental com-
pany issues you with emergency numbers.

Crime
Cuba is a remarkably safe country However,
it is not crime free and sensible precautions
should be taken. To make an insurance claim
for theft or loss, you'll need to make an official report *(denuncia)* to the police.

Right: Cuba calling – but it can take a long time

COMMUNICATIONS AND NEWS

Internet

Cubans are officially allowed access to a Cuban intranet only, but foreigners can access the worldwide web at a growing number of internet points. In many places you'll be asked to show your passport. Telephone lines can be slow and unreliable, so it's always worth writing long e-mails on Word and saving them to a floppy disc in case the connection breaks.

Telephone

Phoning in Cuba can be a confusing business. The country is in the process of digitalizing services, but this is a piecemeal transition. Codes change frequently (especially in Havana).

Within Cuba, the information service (113) is free and helpful.

From abroad If you're phoning from outside Cuba, dial the country code (+53) and then the city code, losing the 0- or 01- from the prefix. Thus Havana would be +53-7; and Santiago would be +53-22.

Domestic calls Inside Cuba, it's more complicated. For interprovincial calls, all numbers except Havana start with 01-. However, on some non-digital private phones, you may have to drop the first '1' and you may only

be able to call neighboring provinces. Don't use any provincial code when phoning within a province, and if you're in the same municipality, it may be that you have to dial

only the last section of the number – perhaps the last four digits. If you're stuck, ask in a hotel or an ETECSA center for help. You'll save a lot of money if you use the Cuban peso phones. There are coin and card versions, although the card versions are often hard to come by. You can make a quick local call for as little as $0.05 *moneda nacional*.

Useful codes Camagüey 0132, Ciego de Avila 0133, Cienfuegos City 01432, Granma 0123, Guantánamo 0121, Havana 07, Holguin 0124 Isla de la Juventud 0161, Las Tunas 0131, Matanzas 0154, Playa Larga 01459, Pinar del Río city 0182, Sancti Spíritus 0141, Santiago de Cuba 0122, Topes de Collantes 0142, Trinidad 01419, Varadero 0145, Villa Clara 0142.

International calls are expensive and cost less from public booths than from hotels – you'll need a dollar phone card, available in $10 and $20 amounts. To dial out, the international prefix is 119 followed by the country code.

Collect calls from a private phone are hideously expensive.

Mail

Stamps can be bought in *moneda nacional*, but in touristy places they'll only sell them in US dollars. A postcard to Europe takes at least two weeks to arrive. Don't post valuable items.

Media

State control of the media is well nigh total.

Newspapers Cubans rely heavily on the official Communist party newspaper, *Granma*, for their knowledge of what's happening on the domestic and international front. There's a daily edition in Spanish; and a weekly version in a number of languages, including English. A limited selection of international magazines are available in the larger tourist hotels.

Television There are two channels on TV, both state-controlled. The more upscale hotels often have cable TV with CNN but not BBC. One of the most entertaining channels is Clave Cubana, which is a Cuban version of MTV showcasing many of the nation's latest talents.

Radio Your best bet is Radio Taíno, 89.1FM.

Above: post your letters here

USEFUL ADDRESSES

Cuban Tourist Board
154 Shaftesbury Ave, London, WC2H 8JT
Tel: 020-7240-6655, Fax: 020-7836-9265
www.cubatravel.cu

1200 Bay Street, Suite 305
Toronto, ON M5R 2A5
Tel: (416) 362-0700, Fax: (416) 362-6799
www.gocuba.ca

Havana Tourist Information Office
Calle 28 No. 303 e/ 3ra. y 5ta. Avenue
Playa. La Habana, Cuba.
Tel: (07) 204-0624, Fax: (07) 204-8164
E-mail: oficturi@ofitur.mit.tur.cu

Infotur – Havana city information
Tel: (07) 862-4586, 333333
www.infotur.cu

Cubanaair
Skyline Unit 49 Limeharbour
London E14 GTS.
Tel: 020-7537-7909, 7747
www.cubanacan.co.uk

Cuban Embassy
167 High Holborn
London, WC1 6PA
Tel: 020-7240-2488, Fax: 020-7836-2602
Consular Section:
15 Grape Street, London WC1
(Mon–Fri 9:30am–12:30pm)

WEBSITES

www.dtcuba.com/eng – Ministry of Tourism.
www.cubaweb.cu – tourism info and news
www.cubalinda.com – info for US citizens
www.cubatravel.cu – tourism website
www.afrocubaweb.com – info on Afro-Cuban heritage and events
www.cubarte.cult.cu – cultural info
www.cubadirecto.com – Cuban products online.

FURTHER READING

Insight Guide: Cuba. Apa Publications, 2004. Comprehensive guidebook, with lavish photographs and detailed maps.
Birds of Cuba by Orlando Garrido & Arturo Kirkconnell (Christopher Helm, UK, 2000)
Cuba From Columbus to Castro and Beyond, by Jaimi Suchlicki (Brasseys Inc; 5th ed. 2002), an insightful and accessible history.
Cuba: The Pursuit of Freedom, by Hugh Thomas. A history from the English invasion of 1762 to the present.
Dirty Havana Trilogy by Pedro Juan Gutiérrez (Faber, 2001), extraordinary tales of sleaze and poverty in post-Soviet Cuba.
Fidel: A Critical Portrait by Tad Szulc (William Morrow, 1986), one of the few good biographies of Castro.
In Focus: Cuba by Simon Calder and Emily Hatchwell (Latin America Bureau, 1999), a good introduction to Cuba and its people.

ACKNOWLEDGEMENTS

All Photography	**Anna Mockford & Nick Bonetti** *except*
37, 42, 45T, 58, 59, 66T, 67, 84, 88,	**Daniel Aeberhard**
12T	**Eduardo Gil**
10, 14	**Richter Library, University of Miami**
79	**Neil Schlecht**
Front cover	**Superstock/Powerstock**
Cartography	**Mapping Ideas Ltd**

The author would like especially to thank Valentina Buonumori – for toughing out crab punctures and sharing the fun of researching the book – as well as Cubana de Aviación, Via Rentacar, Miguel AntonioMuñoz López, Bayamo Armando Rangel Rivero and the Museo Antropológico Montané

credits

INDEX

Register with
HotelClub.com
and get £10!

At **HotelClub.com**, we reward our Members with discounts and free stays in their favourite hotels. As a Member, every booking made by you through **HotelClub.com** will earn you Member Dollars.

When you register, we will credit your account with **£10** which you can use for your next booking! The equivalent of **£10** will be credited in US$ to your Member account (as **HotelClub Member Dollars**). All you need to do is log on to **www.HotelClub.com/pocketguides**. Complete your details, including the Membership Number and Password located on the back of the **HotelClub.com** card.

Over 2.2 million Members already use Member Dollars to pay for all or part of their hotel bookings. Join now and start spending Member Dollars whenever and wherever you want – you are not restricted to specific hotels or dates!

With great savings of up to 60% on over 20,000 hotels across 97 countries, you are sure to find the perfect location for business or pleasure. Happy travels from **HotelClub.com!**